FREDERICK DOUGLASS

FREDERICK DOUGLASS
FOR THE GREAT FAMILY OF MAN

PETER BURCHARD

ATHENEUM BOOKS FOR YOUNG READERS
New York   London   Toronto   Sydney   Singapore

Atheneum Books for Young Readers

An imprint of Simon & Schuster Children's Publishing Division

1230 Avenue of the Americas

New York, New York 10020

Book design by Anne Scatto

The text of this book is set in Bulmer.

Printed in the United States of America

First Edition

2 4 6 8 10 9 7 5 3 1

Library of Congress Cataloging-in-Publication Data

Burchard, Peter.

Frederick Douglass : for the great family of man / by Peter Burchard.

p.   cm.

Includes bibliographical references (p.) and index.

Summary: A biography of the runaway slave who became an abolitionist, a crusader for

women's rights, and an advisor to Abraham Lincoln.

ISBN 1-4169-6752-4

ISBN 13: 978-1-4169-6752-1

1. Douglass, Frederick, 1817?–1895—Juvenile literature. 2. African American abolitionists—Biography—Juvenile literature.

3. Abolitionists—United States—Biography—Juvenile literature. 4. Antislavery movements—United States—History—

19th century—Juvenile literature. [1. Douglass, Frederick, 1817?–1895. 2. Slaves. 3. Abolitionists.

4. African Americans—Biography. 5. Antislavery movements.] I. Title.

E449.D75 B86 2003

973.7(092—dc21

[B]   2001033313

For Jane

TABLE *of* CONTENTS

CONTENTS

ACKNOWLEDGMENTS

Thanks to editor Marcia Marshall for her sage advice and constant loyalty. Thanks to editors Caitlin Van Dusen and Annie Kelley for assistance freely given, and to Arlene Bouras for her tireless and incisive copyediting.

Thanks to Williams College librarian David Pilachowski and his staff for their interest and their help. Thanks to the reference team: Lee Dalzell, Peter Giordano, Christine Menard, and Rebecca Spencer. Many thanks to Circulation Supervisor Jo-Ann Irace and the members of her staff. A special vote of thanks to Walter Komorowski, whose capacity to navigate among the rocks and shoals of the Sea of Electronic Resources never ceases to delight me. Thanks also to Robert Volz and Wayne Hammond, custodians of the Williams College Archives and Special Collections, and Sylvia Kennick Brown and Linda Hall at the Chapin Library.

Thanks to Karl S. Kabelac, the recently retired librarian and archivist at the Department of Rare Books and Special Collections at the University of Rochester. Karl not only rounded up material for me but was kind enough to read and criticize my manuscript, and, in so doing, helped make this a better book than it might otherwise have been.

AUTHOR'S NOTE

Born a slave and later freed, Frederick Douglass was at first primarily concerned with the emancipation of American slaves and the protection and advancement of free black people in America. But his true greatness lay in his concern for all the people of the earth, concern for what he called "the great family of man."

He campaigned for women's rights. He spoke on behalf of Catholics in Ireland. He sympathized with people who had suffered anti-Semitism and he criticized injustices in China and mistreatment of Asian immigrants to the United States. He spoke out for the rights of native peoples. He was among the first to praise his country's "composite nationality."

Douglass was both saint and sinner, but Americans of every color, every faith, owe him a debt of gratitude.

PETER BURCHARD
Williamstown, Massachusetts

"THIS IS THE CAUSE OF

HUMAN BROTHERHOOD AS WELL AS

THE CAUSE OF HUMAN SISTERHOOD,

AND BOTH MUST RISE AND FALL TOGETHER."

—Frederick Douglass

NANTUCKET

O N TUESDAY, August 10, 1841, Frederick Douglass, three years a fugitive from slavery, paced the top deck of the ferry that was taking him from New Bedford to the island of Nantucket.

At twenty-three, he stood above the six-foot mark and, having labored in shipyards in Maryland and Massachusetts, was both broad and muscular. His skin was golden brown. His wide forehead and prominent cheekbones framed dark and penetrating eyes, a broad nose, and a generous mouth. His hands were tough and leathery.

With Douglass on the little steamer was a large and sometimes boisterous crowd of passengers, most of them white, some of them black. All but a few were abolitionists—men and women speaking out against the cruelties of slavery in the South and prejudice and racial violence in the North. Most were firm believers in nonviolence. Earlier that morning, in a strong but peaceful demonstration in New Bedford, Massachusetts, the white majority had gained for their black friends the right to travel with them on the upper deck and in the cabin of the steamer.

Douglass was physically imposing, yet, because he was a runaway, there was something tentative in his manner. He nurtured a vain hope that in such a gathering, he might be inconspicuous. He spoke only when spoken to and, standing on the fringes of the crowd, listened to debates on slavery and abolition, one of which was between a slaveholder from New Orleans and a Massachusetts minister.

Douglass left the crowd, leaned on the rail, and watched several low-lying coastal islands rise up, then disappear in the translucent summer mist. He stared down at the steamer's wake as it fanned out, thinned, and dissolved in the dark waters of Nantucket Sound. As he had in his childhood on the Eastern Shore of Maryland, he paid close attention to the white sails passing—canvas giving life and purpose to the tall ships and the fleets of fishing boats.

Nantucket first appears as a thin violet haze, floating just above the far

A street scene in New Bedford where Douglass and his family lived when he visited Nantucket. Nantucket and New Bedford were almost sister villages. Both were whaling ports and their streets were similar.

horizon. The island, an outpost of a windswept coast, is covered in wild rose and pine and twisted oak. In the nineteenth century, a brightly painted lightship warned the captains of the sailing ships and steamers not to wander from a course well north of Nantucket Shoals, where lay the skeletons of vessels lost in hurricanes and winter storms.

Douglass and the other passengers watched as the ferry made its way between two parallel breakwaters and approached a spindly wharf, where linesmen waited to secure the steamer and where islanders were waving at arriving passengers. Houses and public buildings covered a low ridge above the waterfront. Most of them were shingled structures rendered gray by salt and sun. Some were pink brick with slate roofs and white-painted doors and trim. On the horizon, bright against a dark-blue sky, stood a row of widely separated steeples and windmills.

Douglass had come to Nantucket* to attend an abolitionist convention, but did not intend to speak or to reveal his slave name or his history. For three years, he had toiled night and day, and he hoped that his first visit to Nantucket might serve as a short vacation.

As he stepped down the gangplank, he was painfully aware that—under a federal law passed in 1793—he might be captured and returned to slavery. True, in recent years the law had seldom been enforced in New England, but pressure had begun to build for passage of a stronger law. Douglass later summed up his predicament: "In the northern states, a fugitive slave [was] liable to be hunted at any moment, like a felon, and to be hurled into the terrible jaws of slavery." Indeed, for Douglass, a return to Maryland would almost certainly be followed by banishment to the deep South, from which escape would be almost impossible.

*Nantucket is the name of the island, the county, and the town.

He walked with other members of the party to New Guinea, a neighborhood occupied by free black Americans, Portuguese from the Azores, and Kanakas from the Sandwich Islands—now the islands of Hawaii. These were people who had settled in Nantucket when the whaling industry was at its peak, in the century before. Douglass probably stayed with a family in New Guinea, but in any case, on the night of his arrival and for two days after that, he attended antislavery meetings in an undistinguished building called "the big shop," which served as a meeting place until completion of the Atheneum, six years later.

There he listened to the routine business of the meetings and to vociferous attacks on slavery as practiced in America: the sale and purchase of black people, the breaking up of families, the whippings and related cruelties that were part and parcel of an institution seen by Douglass as degrading to slaveholders, as well as to their human property, an evil that had undermined and was threatening to destroy democracy.

Most white people present, some of them from privileged families, knew black people only as inferiors—as servants, laborers, and craftsmen. More important, they had never witnessed slavery. They were men and women of good will, but most of them took a condescending or at best paternalistic view of both slaves and free black Americans.

It was on the evening of the second day that Douglass suddenly, almost rudely, found himself in the limelight. Unknown to him, there was someone in the auditorium who had heard him speak not long before. Years later, he recalled, "Mr. William C. Coffin, a prominent abolitionist in those days of trial, had heard me speaking to my colored friends, in the little school-house on Second Street in New Bedford, where we worshiped."

At the convention in Nantucket, Coffin sought Douglass out and invited him to make a few remarks. Douglass agreed, but not yet a seasoned speaker, he was terrified at the prospect of addressing such a large and distinguished audience: "I trembled in every limb. . . . It was with the utmost difficulty that I could stand erect, or that I could command and articulate two words without hesitation and stammering."

Even as a little boy, Douglass had been noticed as possessing keen intelligence; but it was not his wit that made him stand out that day in Nantucket, it was his emotion bursting forth out of a clear memory of the life that he had led as a young slave in his native Maryland.

Nobody took notes on his speech, and Douglass remembered nothing of its content. But it was clear that his excitement and confusion were contagious. When he stepped down from the platform, the audience broke into wild applause. Stunned, then elated, Douglass went back to his seat.

No sooner had he settled down than a small, pale, balding man in his mid-thirties, wearing wire-rimmed glasses stood up and moved swiftly

William Lloyd Garrison's *Liberator* was the most durable antislavery newspaper of them all. It was "meat and drink" to Douglass. After its initial publication on January 1, 1831, the paper sported several mastheads. This one was its last and most familiar.

Our Country is the World, our Countrymen are all Mankind.

down the aisle toward the podium. As the man began to speak, tears glistened in his eyes. This, Douglass knew, was William Lloyd Garrison, the most conspicuous of New England abolitionists, publisher of a weekly paper called *The Liberator*. Douglass had heard Garrison address an antislavery gathering in New Bedford. He had read *The Liberator* and had marveled at its editorials, some of which attacked the United States Constitution and called into question the morality of commerce in both the North and the South. "The paper," he wrote later, "became my meat and my drink." It set his soul "all on fire." Its attacks on intolerance and slavery "sent a thrill of joy through my soul, such as I had never felt before!"

The short speech Douglass made that Wednesday evening has been lost, but Garrison, who had spent most of his adult life fighting slavery, said of Douglass's demonstration of emotion, "I think I never hated slavery so intensely as at that moment."

Douglass remembered, "Mr. Garrison followed me, taking me as his text." Even those who knew Garrison and had heard him often "were astonished." His speech, Douglass thought, "was an effort of unequaled power, sweeping down, like a very tornado, every opposing barrier."

Garrison raised emotion in the hall to a high pitch. At first, speaking quietly, he asked, "Have we been listening to a *thing,* a piece of property, or a *man?*

"A man! A man!"

Garrison raised his voice as he asked, "And should such a man be held a slave in a republican and Christian land?"

Almost in a single voice, the audience shouted, "Never!"

Douglass hadn't mentioned his slave name or the names of people he had known in Maryland, but it was clear that in speaking as he had, he had risked being jailed in Massachusetts and returned to slavery. Garrison spoke of this risk, spoke of Douglass as a man of strength and talent; then, in an insistent voice, he asked, "Shall such a man be sent back to slavery from the soil of old Massachusetts?"

The people in the crowded hall gave voice to their outrage. "Never!"

Douglass saw that he had had a powerful effect on Garrison, and Garrison knew that Douglass could be useful to his cause. "It was at once deeply impressed upon my mind, that, if Mr. Douglass could be persuaded to consecrate his time and talents to the . . . anti-slavery enterprise, a powerful impetus would be given to it, and a stunning blow at the same time inflicted on northern prejudice against a colored complexion."

Douglass's halting speech, his deep embarrassment, his eloquence—all duly noted by the veteran Garrison and by others in the hall—marked a momentous turning point in the life of the young fugitive. Later, Douglass said, "Here opened upon me a new life—a life for which I had had no preparation."

Douglass may have had no formal preparation for his new life, but his years in bondage were to give him an advantage over white crusaders and most of their free black counterparts. This advantage would, in time, make some of them jealous.

2

THOSE SONGS STILL FOLLOW ME

DOUGLASS WAS born in 1818, in the month of February—day unknown. He was part of a large family rooted in the soil, the creeks, and the estuaries of the Eastern Shore of Maryland, a narrow L-shaped strip of land on a peninsula that lies between Delaware Bay and the shallow waters of the Chesapeake.

Because he belonged to the long-established Bailey family and because his father was unknown, he inherited his mother's surname. In the only record of his birth, he is listed as "Frederick Augustus, son of Harriott Feby 1818." His mother, whose first name was elsewhere spelled "Harriet," chose to call her second son Frederick Augustus Washington Bailey. Years later, after he escaped from Maryland, he changed his name to Frederick Douglass.

Frederick's maternal grandfather, Isaac Bailey, was a free man, a sawyer: a craftsman who cut and trimmed hardwood and pine. He sold the products of his hands to carpenters and cabinetmakers, so he had money of his own. Frederick's grandmother, called "Aunt Betsey," might as well have been born free, so much freedom did she have. But his mother, as the daughter of a woman who was technically a slave, was anything but free.

Frederick, who could only speculate about his father, knew his mother only slightly, but would remember her as tall, dark-skinned, and beautiful. She was "sedate and dignified." Harriet—counted as an asset among mules and oxen, cows and sheep and chickens, and rated as less valuable than a dray horse—bent her back from dawn to dusk to hoe and seed and harvest wheat and to plant and bring in corn. At the same time, she was obliged to give birth to a brood of healthy children, who in time would increase her master's fortune.

Most members of the Bailey clan were born near Tuckahoe Creek, on Holme Hill Farm, which was owned by their master, Aaron Anthony, who, it was rumored, might have been Frederick's father.* "Slavery," Frederick was to say, "does away with fathers, as it does away with families."

Frederick was the fourth of seven children—two boys and five girls— but his life was so arranged that he seldom saw or had a chance to know and love his brothers and his sisters. His mother, who was forced to give him up when she finished nursing him, soon became a ghostly loving presence, then a distant and romantic memory.

It was Frederick's happy childhood years and a generous measure of good fortune that sustained him in his years of abject slavery. As a child, Frederick lived with Aunt Betsey, who raised scores of children while their mothers spent their daylight hours working and their nights recuperating from the rigors of their toil. Aunt Betsey was as tall and dignified as her daughter Harriet. Born two years before the signing of Thomas Jefferson's Declaration of Independence—a document that had no immediate effect on the life of any slave—she was in her forties when her grandson Frederick came

---

*As a youth, Frederick may or may not have believed that Anthony was his father. Later, he wrote, "My father was a white man, or nearly white." In his final memoir, he refused to speculate, saying only, "Of my father I know nothing."

Maryland slaves at work. This painting, done in 1805, illustrates what Douglass saw years later, as a child. Both men and women bent their backs six days a week, from dawn to dusk.

to live with her. She was a skillful gardener and a practiced fisherwoman. She knew how to bait a line and take a crab and how to find an oyster bed.

Aunt Betsey's modest cabin near the Tuckahoe was a sort of nursery, where slave children lived in blissful ignorance of what lay in store for them. There Frederick went barefoot, rinsed his single, roughly woven garment in the creek, and dried it in the sun; but soon after it was given to him, it became torn and tattered and was not to be replaced for many months. None of Aunt Betsey's children starved, but they lived mostly on cornmeal. Now and then, Betsey blessed her favorite grandson with a sweet potato or a morsel of crabmeat.

His mother must sometimes have watched him from afar, must have taken pleasure in his antics, must have noticed his intelligence developing. But as often as she might have longed to speak to him and nurture him, she found only isolated opportunities to do so.

Somehow Frederick learned that when he was six or seven, he would have to leave his grandmother. "The fact is, such was my dread of leaving the little cabin, that I wished to remain little forever, for I knew the taller I grew the shorter my stay. The old cabin, with its rail floor and rail bedsteads upstairs, and its clay floor downstairs, and its dirt chimney, and windowless sides . . . and the hole curiously dug in front of the fire-place, beneath which grandmammy placed the sweet potatoes to keep them from the frost, was MY HOME—the only home I ever had; and I loved it."

If one thing marked Frederick as an individual, it was his capacity to contemplate the mysteries of his childhood world. "Down in a little valley, not far from grandmammy's cabin, stood Mr. Lee's mill, where the people came often in large numbers to get their corn ground. It was a water-mill; and I never shall be able to tell the many things thought and felt, while I sat on the bank and watched that mill, and the turning of that ponderous wheel."

In his grandmother's yard, he discovered that the stars were more than holes in a dark-blue sheet of paper. He learned that tender roots stirred underneath the surface of the soil long before the spring rains brought forth grass and vegetables and flowers.

With a bent pin, Frederick fished in the mill pond. His was a carefree life, but "in all my sports and plays, and in spite of them, there would, occasionally, come the painful foreboding that I was not long to remain there, and that I must soon be called away to the home of old master." Although he knew that someday he must leave Holme Hill Farm, his

This photograph, taken thirty years after emancipation, shows a cabin like the one occupied by Aunt Betsey.

grandmother left him unprepared for the journey and the loneliness that would follow it.

When the fearsome day came, he was anxious but was trustful. He and his grandmother set out on a summer morning. Even as they started down the long and dusty road, she refused to talk about the purpose of their journey. It was only later that he understood that her reserve was necessary, "for, could I have known all, I should have given Grandmother some trouble in getting me started. As it was, I was helpless, and she—dear woman!—led me along by the hand."

She had walked to the Wye River many times and reckoned that the distance was about twelve miles. Soon she saw that her grandson was footsore, and now and then, she picked him up and carried him.

His grandmother knew that Frederick was exceptional. No doubt she guessed that his intelligence would make it difficult, if not impossible, for him to be a docile and compliant slave. In any case, she was soon to introduce him to a world that would dazzle him and frighten him—a world ruled by a man named Edward Lloyd V, who was a demigod to the slaves on the Wye Plantation and on his other holdings on the Eastern Shore. Lloyd was then in his forties. He was tall, white-haired, and handsome. He was always tastefully attired, in the manner of an English country gentleman. His lips were thin, his eyes blue, and his expression merciless.

Lloyd's mansion—referred to by his slaves as the Great House—was the center of his empire. It was a large white-painted structure, with a wing on either side and surrounded by dependencies—smaller buildings, occupied by Lloyd's overseers and his slaves, and separate kitchens, dairies, greenhouses, hen and turkey houses, a pigeon house, and summerhouse. Lloyd's stable, almost as elegant as the Great House, held a string of thoroughbreds, each one prized as highly as a member of his family.

Lloyd's forebears, who had come from Wales at least two hundred years before, had accumulated a large fortune through efficient use of slaves and by making advantageous marriages. At first, the Lloyds depended on the cultivation of tobacco, but when their tobacco crops began to fail, they shifted their attention to wheat farming and raising sheep. They grew corn as food for animals and for the slaves. The family owned a flock of some seven hundred sheep, and during Frederick's years at what is now called Wye House, Lloyd was by far the most successful farmer in the state of Maryland and among the most successful in America.

Although most of the Baileys belonged to widower Aaron Anthony, Anthony worked for Lloyd. He and his family lived on the Lloyd estate. So, in effect, most of Anthony's overseers and field hands really worked for Lloyd.

As his grandmother led Frederick toward the Lloyd estate, he knew almost nothing of the world he was about to enter, a world where there would be no grandmother to turn to in times of pain or disappointment, a place where complaining of injustice not only would do no good but might worsen his predicament. Frederick walked in ignorance, but the sad expression on his grandmother's face caused him to conjure up imaginary dangers. Passing through a somber wood, he expected monsters to emerge from shadows. "Several old logs and stumps imposed upon me, and got themselves taken for wild beasts. I could see their legs, eyes, and ears."

It was not until that afternoon that the two travelers reached "the dreaded end of the journey." The first sign was a glimpse of open fields and a vast garden tended by at least a dozen women who were chattering and singing mournfully. Later Frederick said that the memory of the singing made his eyes fill with tears. "Those songs still follow me."

His grandmother pointed out "a group of children of many colors; black, brown, copper colored, and nearly white." She guided him to a brick house, near the Great House. It was there that Frederick's master, Aaron Anthony, lived with his surviving daughter, Lucretia, and her husband, Thomas Auld. There, in Anthony's large kitchen, Frederick was to spend his first night worlds away from his grandmother's cabin.

Frederick had the impression of a closely manicured establishment—a carefully tended kitchen garden, rows of fruit trees in an orchard, and beyond the orchard, sheep and lambs clustered in the shade of an oak tree. He heard the merry ringing of a blacksmith's hammer and the whinny of a horse. These pleasant sights and sounds gave no comfort to a boy who was clinging desperately to his grandmother's skirts, a boy who sensed that his life away from home would hold unexpected terrors for him.

"Affectionately patting me on the head, and exhorting me to be a good

Wye House is much as it was when it was owned by Edward Lloyd V. During his stay at the Lloyd Plantation, Frederick lived in the wood-frame kitchen of a brick house behind Wye House and inhabited by Aaron Anthony and members of his family. Anthony owned Frederick and was probably his father.

boy, Grandmamma told me to go and play with the little children. 'They are kin to you,' said she." She pointed out and named six of his cousins, and she introduced him to his older brother, Perry, and two sisters, Sarah and Eliza, all of whom were strangers to the boy who had lived his life by the brown waters of the Tuckahoe. Later, he lamented, "My poor mother, like many other slave-women, had *many children* but NO FAMILY!"

In spite of his anxiety, Frederick was curious about his siblings. At first, he was inclined to play with them, but was afraid that his grandmother might go back to Holme Hill Farm without him. At last, he went to the backyard and joined the other children. Later, he remembered, "*Play*, however, I did not, but stood with my back against the wall."

At last, one of the other children came to him and, with a sadistic smile, exclaimed, "Fed, Fed! grandmammy gone! grandmammy gone!"

Terrified and heartbroken, Frederick "fell upon the ground, and wept a boy's bitter tears, refusing to be comforted. My brother and sisters came around me, and said, 'Don't cry,' and gave me peaches and pears, but I flung them away and refused all their kindly advances. I had never been deceived before; and I felt not only grieved at parting—as I supposed forever—with my grandmother, but indignant that a trick had been played upon me."

Following what he called his "first introduction to the realities of slavery," he kept to himself until sundown, then curled up in a corner of the kitchen, where he slept.

3

OH, HAVE MERCY!

I T WAS a sign of Frederick's generosity of spirit that he could sympathize with Aaron Anthony, a man who sometimes smiled at him and other times regarded him without compassion and did things that led Frederick to regard him as a monster.

As an adult, Frederick wrote a poignant paragraph about the man. His words paint a portrait of someone who had so long been ashamed of what he was and how he lived that he had all but lost his mind. "Old master very early impressed me with the idea that he was an unhappy man. Even to my child's eye, he wore a troubled, and at times, haggard aspect. His strange movements excited my curiosity, and awakened my compassion. He seldom walked along without muttering to himself; and he occasionally stormed about, as if defying an army of invisible foes. . . . Most of his leisure was spent in walking, cursing, and gesticulating, like one possessed of a demon. . . . He was a wretched man, at war with his own soul, and with all the world around him."

He was called "Captain" Anthony because, when he was younger, he had been the master of the Lloyd family's schooner, the *Elizabeth and Ann,* a handsome vessel that had taken members of the family, guests, house servants, and cargo to and from the Lloyd townhouse in Annapolis. The *Elizabeth and Ann* had since been sold and replaced by the even more impressive *Sally Lloyd.*

Lloyd had once respected Aaron Anthony, but Anthony had fallen into careless ways. He was often drunk and incapable of working, and Lloyd treated him as he might have treated a paid servant.

Edward Lloyd V, master of the plantation where Douglass spent several years as a child.

Lloyd's life was organized so that he was isolated from the rank injustices that enabled him to live in luxury. He seldom talked to any slave other than his grooms and his house servants. He spoke to his stableboys only to deliver short commands or complain about imperfect maintenance of tack or improper grooming of his favorite mounts. He spoke to Anthony, who, in turn, spoke to overseers, all of whom used tried and trusted methods to control the slaves.

At the pinnacle of the slave society were the house servants. These privileged slaves were chosen for good looks, intelligence, and loyalty. They wore spotless uniforms, were trained to exhibit perfect manners and to serve submissively. They ate fresh vegetables and meat, while their sisters and their brothers lived on meager rations of cornmeal. Most house servants, far from taking pity on field hands, looked down on them and called them "niggers."

During the long days of summer, Lloyd entertained other planters who lived in his neighborhood and close friends and admirers from Annapolis and Baltimore. On gala weekends, well before sunup, slaves who had been trained as cooks prepared the produce gathered from the kitchen gardens and the arbors, glazed the hams and braised the beef, plucked the wild birds and domestic foul.

Lloyd's guests were brought up in a carriage from his landing on the Wye and climbed a set of steps to a portico supported by slim Doric columns. There, they were welcomed at a wide front door opened by a liveried servant. Lloyd's white linen tablecloths were set with the finest crystal and the best of the Lloyd silverware. At special dinners, the domestic bill of fare was augmented by French wines and cheeses, and sweetmeats and liqueurs from Spain and Portugal.

Frederick's life, in the peculiar world of Lloyd and Anthony, was ruled by the sadistic practices of a black woman who took care of the children at Wye House. "Aunt Katy," she was called. Only once did anyone come between Frederick and Aunt Katy's cruelty.

All his life, Frederick cherished a clear memory of his mother's visits to him. Although she worked the fields at Holme Hill Farm from dawn to dusk, several times as the shadows lengthened on the paths and in the wood, her hunger for the sight of her young son was so acute that she found the energy to walk twelve miles to spend half an hour with him. Perhaps she would sit down beside him, sing to him, and watch him as his breathing grew more regular and he drifted into sleep. All his life, Frederick knew that "a true mother's heart was hers." As an older man, he wrote, "I take few steps in life, without feeling her presence."

One February morning, Aunt Katy gave Frederick a small portion of cornmeal mush and gave him no other food all day long. He was brave, but his stoicism dwindled with the coming of twilight. "Sundown came, but *no bread,* and, in its stead, there came the threat, with a scowl well suited to its terrible import, that she 'meant to *starve the life out of me!*'"

"Brandishing her knife, she chopped off the heavy slices for the other children, and put the loaf away, muttering, all the while, her savage designs." Frederick still hoped for a miracle. "Against this disappointment, for I was expecting that [she] would relent at last, I made an extra effort to maintain my dignity; but when I saw all the other children around me with merry and satisfied faces, I could stand it no longer. I went out behind the house, and cried like a fine fellow!"

By the time he went back in, the other children had gone out to play. When Aunt Katy turned her back, he took a few grains from an ear of corn and roasted them. He was just about to eat them, when he saw his mother standing in the doorway. Harriet, sensing that her son was miserable, picked him up and held him tightly in her arms. Questioning Aunt Katy, she found out exactly what had happened. His mother proved herself more than a match for the cowardly, sadistic woman. "There was pity in her glance at me, and a fiery indignation at Aunt Katy."

Hoping that their master, heartless as he might be, wouldn't stand for cruelty to one so young, she told Aunt Katy she would tell him what was happening. She gave her son a heart-shaped ginger cake. Her anger gathered like a summer storm and she gave Aunt Katy a tongue-lashing. Frederick remembered, "I was victorious, and well off for the moment; prouder, on my mother's knee, than a king upon his throne. But my triumph was short. I dropped off to sleep, and waked in the morning only to find my mother gone." However, he had seen that he was not just a child "but *somebody's* child."

Not long after this last visit with his mother, Frederick learned that she had died. If she had asked to see him, her request had been denied. Later, he wrote bitterly, "The bond-woman lives as a slave, and is left to die as a beast. . . . Her grave is, as the grave of the dead at sea, unmarked, and without stone or stake."

In childhood, Frederick had no opportunity to learn to read. For a short time, he was sent to the school of Doctor Isaac Cooper, where the children learned to parrot the Lord's Prayer but were never taught the meaning of its words. Cooper carried a long switch and, sitting on a high stool, towered over his small pupils. When a child was inattentive, Cooper's switch whistled through the air and found its mark. "I was often a truant when the time for attending the praying and flogging of Doctor Isaac Cooper came on."

At the Great House, Frederick not only had no opportunity to learn to speak in common English but was encouraged to communicate in a dialect that at first was foreign to him. For example, if somebody asked him who he was, he was expected to reply, "Cap'n Ant'ney Fed." If he was asking who another slave belonged to, he was supposed to say, "Oo you dem long to?"

It was Frederick's natural curiosity that saved him from abysmal ignorance. His cousin Tom, who worked aboard the *Sally Lloyd*, sailed frequently to Baltimore and brought back trinkets from the fabled seaport. Although Tom stuttered mightily, Frederick urged him to describe the city and was patient as he struggled through his stories. With Tom's fractured visions dancing in his mind, Frederick sometimes found his way to a bank above the Wye or walked to a point of land overlooking the Miles River, so that he could watch the barges and sailboats taking people to Annapolis or Baltimore or to distant, as yet unimagined, places.

Frederick's impishness and charm came in handy in his constant search for food. Noticing his desperation, people working in the Great

House kitchen gave him hunks of bread that they had soaked in chicken stock. Sometimes he was given a substantial meal and words of encouragement. "Never mind, honey. Better day comin'." Other times, he took scraps of meat from cats and dogs.

Frederick later wrote that skin color made no difference to a child. In any case, it seems that Daniel—Lloyd's youngest son—was unaware of racial differences. The two boys became close friends, though it was understood, at least by their seniors, that their friendship must end soon.

While Frederick played in and near the Great House, he still slept in a closet in Aunt Katy's kitchen. His mother's threats notwithstanding, Aunt Katy kept on treating him with scorn and was often cruel to him.

On the Lloyd plantation, Frederick saw the raw and scabrous face of slavery. A cousin, who lived and worked at Holme Hill Farm, came one day to the kitchen. "The poor girl, on her arrival at our house, presented a most pitiable appearance." She had made the familiar twelve-mile journey bleeding from the many wounds inflicted by her overseer. Her neck and shoulders were covered with welts and the "cowardly wretch had dealt her a blow on the head with a hickory club, which cut a horrible gash." She came seeking mercy but found none. Anthony sent her back to her sadistic overseer.

Not old enough to go to work as a field hand, Frederick did light work around the house. "The most I had

Early nineteenth-century wood engraving symbolizing the relationship between a master and his slave.

to do, was to drive up the cows in the evening, to keep the front yard clean, and to perform small errands for my young mistress."

His "young mistress" was Lucretia Auld, who later helped shape his destiny. Lucretia was the daughter of the distressed and unstable Aaron Anthony. Married to Thomas Auld, she had a daughter of her own named Amanda. All three lived with Anthony. Lucretia was a tenderhearted woman and her daughter, then a child of four or five, had inherited her mother's temperament.

One day, following a vicious fight with another boy his age, Frederick came in from the yard with a deep cut on his forehead. Aunt Katy gave him a cold glance and suggested that he'd better keep away "from dem Lloyd niggers."

But Lucretia, who was sitting in the kitchen, seeing that Frederick's wound was bleeding freely, filled a basin with springwater, washed the cut, and bound his head with a clean white length of linen. After that, she and Frederick were good friends.

Also in Aunt Katy's kitchen, he was witness to a tragic series of events. His Aunt Esther, who like him belonged to Aaron Anthony, was in her teens. She was beautiful and perhaps mature beyond her years. Beauty, Frederick was to learn, was a curse to any woman slave of any age. Esther was in love with a young man owned by and named after Edward Lloyd V. Ned was a fine figure of a man and he loved Esther desperately.

Some Maryland slaveholders would have sanctioned marriage between two attractive slaves, or at least would have tolerated their association, but because Esther was so beautiful, Anthony lusted after her himself and was driven to the depths of jealousy. He tried to discourage the affair, but Ned and Esther's passion was too deep to be denied, and against Anthony's orders and perhaps against Lloyd's wishes, they met often after dark.

When Anthony failed in his initial efforts to discourage the romance, he took sterner measures. His motives, Frederick later wrote, "were as abhorrent as his methods were foolish and contemptible." Indeed, in this case, his behavior couldn't be explained as necessary to a system Frederick knew that he was bound to serve.

One morning, shortly after dawn, Frederick, sleeping in his closet, was awakened by a piercing shriek. He pressed his cheek against a rough plank of the door and, peering through a generous crack, saw Esther hanging in a perilous position. Her wrists were tied to a high beam. Stripped to the waist, she was standing on a bench, on tiptoe, while Anthony, holding a long cowhide lash, stood behind her, savoring his power over one so comely and so delicate.*

The girl's shoulders, Frederick noticed, were plump, tender, and unmarked. At last, Anthony raised his arm and brought his lash down on her back, raising a long, ugly welt. She cried out, *"Oh! have mercy!"* Then, when Anthony paused a moment, she gave in. She moaned, *"I won't do so no more."*

Her cries and her entreaties did no more than intensify her master's wrath. Anthony whipped her more than thirty times, and then, breathing heavily and swearing, he took out his knife and cut her down.

The testimony of a slave was useless, but Frederick believed that if Anthony discovered he had been a witness to the lashing, he, too, would feel his master's wrath. "I was hushed, terrified, and stunned."

Before the year was out, Esther had a baby by Ned Roberts. Probably because Esther's presence was a constant taunt, Anthony sold her and her child to a slave dealer.

---

*The practice of tying a woman to a branch or beam to prepare her for a whipping was apparently not uncommon in Maryland or in parts of the Deep South. English actress Fanny Kemble wrote of such an episode in her *Journal of a Residence on a Georgian Plantation in 1838–1839,* published first in 1863.

These sorts of injustices prompted Frederick to question slavery, something he had never done before. Why were some people free and others not? Why was his grandfather free and why had his mother not been free? Frederick had heard an overseer say, "It's worth but half a cent to kill a nigger, and a half a cent to bury him." Why was the life of a black person— a man, woman, child—less valuable than the life of a white person?

In the summer of 1825, Frederick's aunt Jenny and her husband, Noah, escaped from the Eastern Shore. These were people who were living quietly with their son and daughter. Probably because they knew that they were destined to be sold and therefore separated, they left their children with Aunt Betsey and contrived somehow to go north along the slim peninsula shared by the states of Maryland and Delaware, and escape to a free state.

$150 REWARD.

RANAWAY from the Subscriber, living in Talbot county, Maryland, on Saturday the twenty-seventh instant, negro man Noah, 26 years old, about 5 feet 10 or 11 inches high, stout and black, has very full ill shaped feet and is clumsy in his walk; negro Jenny, 26 years old, of a chesnut colour, middling size, and a well shaped woman. These negroes I raised myself, and intended to give them their freedom.

I will give one hundred dollars for the man and fifty for the woman if delivered to me, or so secured that I shall get them.

Sep 6. W   AARON ANTHONY.

Advertisement for recapture of Frederick's aunt and uncle. They made good their escape in 1825.

Anthony didn't have so many slaves that he could overlook the loss of two of them. At first, he declared his determination to pursue them, then instead placed a notice in a local newspaper, offering fifty dollars for the woman and one hundred dollars for the man. If the couple hoped that they might someday be reunited with their children, Anthony made sure that they would not. He sold both children to an Alabama trader.

4

LOOK UP, CHILD

IT WAS Lucretia Auld who told Frederick that her father had decided to send him to Baltimore to live with her husband's brother Hugh. In fact, it may well have been Lucretia who prevailed upon him to do so. In any case, at the age of eight, the boy began a life that would enable him to acquire some useful skills, avoid the cruel existence of a field hand, and diminish the real possibility that he would be sent in chains to New Orleans.

And it was Lucretia who prepared Frederick for his journey. She told him to scrub himself, head to toe, so as to remove what she called the "scurf" of the plantation. She asked him to give close attention to his callused feet and knees and gave him a good pair of trousers and a clean white shirt.

So it was that Frederick left the Eastern Shore on a Saturday in March of 1826. He sailed aboard the *Sally Lloyd* with a large flock of sheep that was destined for a slaughterhouse in Baltimore. As the boat moved slowly down the Wye, he must have thought about the people on the Eastern Shore who had loved him and befriended him. He knew he had lost his mother. It saddened him to have lost touch with his grandmother. His friendship with Daniel Lloyd had been short. He knew that he would miss Lucretia Auld, but hoped that she might visit Baltimore and call on him. In fact, Lucretia, who was ailing, was to die within a year.

Frederick later wrote that, as he left the Lloyd plantation, he felt not a shadow of regret. "My strong aversion to the great house farm was not owing to my own personal suffering, but the daily suffering of others, and to the certainty that I must, sooner or later, be placed under the barbarous rule of an overseer."

The wind freshened as they left the Wye. Sailing down the Miles River into Eastern Bay and northwest in the Chesapeake, Frederick stood up in the bow and watched the ships in the main channel, some of them heading toward the lower reaches of the Chesapeake.

Late that afternoon, the *Sally Lloyd* entered the small harbor at Annapolis and tied up at Taylor's Dock. Frederick had never seen a town of any size, and the beautiful but modest capital of Maryland was, to him, as impressive as a large and distant European seaport. The town was dominated by its statehouse, which stood on a rise surrounded by attendant buildings.

Frederick had no chance to go ashore. When the *Sally Lloyd* left Annapolis and sailed again toward Baltimore, he probably had some supper, found a bunk, and slept the night away.

The boat arrived in Baltimore Sunday morning. If Annapolis had begun to open Frederick's eyes, Baltimore must have dazzled the young slave. Surrounded by a ring of gentle hills and the clustered buildings of the city, the vast harbor was alive with sailing vessels—sloops much like the *Sally Lloyd,* schooners, packet ships, armed brigantines—and all manner of small pleasure boats, workboats, and rowing scows.

The *Sally Lloyd* docked at Smith's Wharf, near Pratt Street, and Frederick was pressed into service to help drive the sheep to market, then he was led by a deckhand down dusty lanes and cobbled avenues toward his new home in the Fells Point district. As he walked through the streets of Baltimore, he was surprised to see large numbers of free black people walking with an air of confidence, their heads held high, some of them dressed as well as any servant on the Lloyd plantation.

In the doorway of a modest wood-frame house in Happy Alley, just off Aliceanna Street, he met people who, for twelve years, were to be the central figures in his life. Hugh Auld was younger than his brother Thomas. He had a narrow, pallid face, a long, thin nose, and lips set in a bloodless line. Sophia Auld at once put Frederick at ease. Her son Tommy held her

Annapolis, Maryland, dominated by the State House, was the first city Frederick ever saw.

hand while she spoke softly, introducing him to Frederick. She told Tommy that Frederick would take care of him.

Frederick climbed up to a loft above the kitchen, where Sophia had made up a bed for him on a mattress stuffed with straw. That evening, he sat down to supper with the Aulds, scarcely able to believe that, for a while at least, he would be treated as a member of a family. He enjoyed his first full meal and went to bed between clean sheets, covered with a woolen blanket.

In the days that followed his arrival, Frederick started to explore the streets that surrounded Happy Alley. He discovered that Fells Point was a shipbuilding district. He learned that Hugh Auld worked in a shipyard and hoped soon to start a shipyard of his own.

Frederick watched the final stages of the building of an eighteen-hundred-ton warship and was present at her launching. The May 12, 1826, edition of the *Baltimore American* reported that "the ship moved toward her destined element with an easy and gradually accelerated motion, and having made one plunge of obeisance to old Neptune, rose majestically upon the water, amidst the shouts in admiration of the assembled thousands. We believe that a more beautiful and better-managed launch has never been made."

Such a sight must have broadened Frederick's sense of the near miracles that people could perform if they worked together; but perhaps the greatest wonder he encountered in Fells Point was the love and sympathy of the woman he called "Miss Sophia."

What sort of woman could treat Frederick as a second son? Sophia Auld had been an artisan—a weaver of fine woolens—but by the time that Frederick came to her, she found little time to sit before a loom; she was by then a housewife and a mother. Her parents, who were working-class white people, had encouraged her to believe that slavery was a crime against humanity. Until her husband noticed her behavior and reminded her that Frederick was a slave, it did not occur to her to treat Frederick any differently than she treated her son Tommy. After dark, when Frederick heard the sounds of slaves being taken to a wharf to be put aboard a slave ship that was bound for the Deep South, she revealed to him that the rattle of their chains and the shouts of the slave drivers pained her as much as they frightened him.

Sophia Auld was indeed a sympathetic woman, but so long had Frederick been intimidated that he seldom found it possible to face white people. When he failed to look Sophia in the eye, she said gently, "Look up, child; don't be afraid."

As Frederick began to realize what it meant to be illiterate, he wondered how he might begin to learn to read. At first, he coaxed and tricked white boys who went to school into teaching him some of the letters of the alphabet. He learned how to read street signs.

Frederick's master Aaron Anthony died on the Lloyd Plantation on November 14, 1826. Slaves—like land, houses, furniture, and animals—were property, and when a slaveholder died, his slaves were distributed among his heirs or sold and the proceeds portioned out. Anthony had written no last will and testament. He probably intended to let Frederick stay with Hugh Auld in Baltimore, but nobody could prove this.

When he died, Anthony had three children—Andrew, Richard, and Lucretia. But when the time came to divide his property, Lucretia, too, had died. It was ruled that her portion of her father's holdings go to her husband, Thomas Auld, who by then had left the Lloyd Plantation and was managing a general store and post office in St. Michaels—a village on the Eastern Shore.

So that it would be possible to put a value on the twenty-nine slaves owned by Aaron Anthony, all must be assembled at Holme Hill Farm. Word came to Hugh Auld, in Baltimore, that Frederick must be sent back to the place where he had been born.

Frederick had spent nearly nine months with the Aulds in Baltimore. They were his only family. Even Master Thomas, who was not at all a loving person, had developed an affection for him. As Frederick stood forlornly on the afterdeck of the *Wildcat,* Sophia Auld burst into tears and Tommy, not quite understanding what was happening but knowing that his friend was leaving him, cried bitterly.

The *Wildcat,* far from living up to its ferocious name, was a slow vessel, built so that she could navigate the shallow creeks and estuaries

Baltimore from Federal Hill, as it was when Douglass knew it.

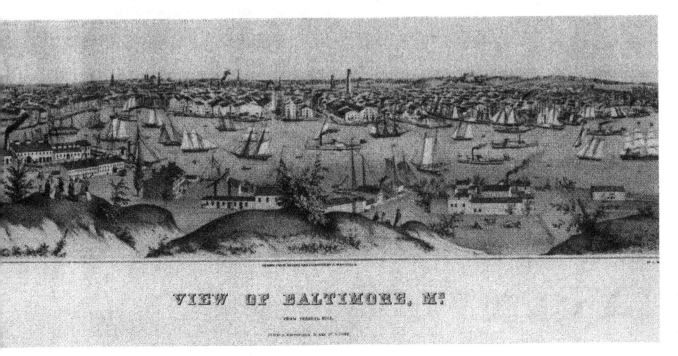

VIEW OF BALTIMORE, M?

of the Eastern Shore. A full day and a night went by before the *Wildcat* reached her destination, giving Frederick ample time to brood about what might lie in store for him. Until he had heard about his aunt's escape, he had never thought of freedom. Now he knew that there was such a thing as a free state. He understood that if a slave was smart enough and strong enough he might map a way to freedom. "Young as I was," he later wrote, "I was already, in spirit and purpose, a fugitive from slavery."

The *Wildcat* bypassed Eastern Bay and made its way up the broad and often shallow Choptank River to the mouth of the Tuckahoe, where she anchored. A member of the *Wildcat*'s crew took Frederick in a creaky rowboat to a landing on the west shore of the Tuckahoe and walked with him to his grandmother's cabin.

Because she had every reason to believe that she would stay at Holme Hill Farm and raise children not yet born, then say good-bye to them, his grandmother must have had an unsentimental outlook toward all but a few of her wards. But she could not deny her love for Frederick, nor could he deny his love for her. So when he walked across her yard, she came out and looked at him with undisguised affection, then embraced him.

At Holme Hill Farm, Frederick saw familiar faces. He might well have taken pleasure from the suffering of Aunt Katy, who was there with her three sons and her daughter, but he was a remarkably forgiving person. At the farm, he saw his older brother, Perry, and his older sisters, Sarah and Eliza, and he greeted cousin Tom. He talked with his aunt Prissy—plump, attractive, and good-natured. He took a special interest in a child named Harriet, who he thought might have been his mother's child.

Andrew Anthony, who was thirty at the time, was a weak and often drunken man, someone who was capable of unbridled cruelty. Soon after all were gathered at the farm, Andrew turned his wrath on Perry, who was no more than fifteen. Andrew's face was flaming red as he grabbed Perry by the throat and shoved him hard against a wall. Perry slumped and Andrew, standing over him, drove the sharp toe of his boot into Perry's unprotected head. Perry, blood gushing from his nose and ears, lay still, while Frederick and the others, afraid to offer help or even sympathy, stood by, thinking he might die.

Then came the day when all the people who had belonged to Aaron Anthony were prodded into a long line. Frederick's own description of the sight, written later, tells the story. There were gathered "men and women, young and old, married and single . . . in open contempt of their humanity. . . . How vividly, at that moment, did the brutalizing power of slavery flash before me! . . .

"Our destiny was now to be *fixed for life,* and we had no more voice in the decision of the question, than the oxen and cows that stood chewing at the hay-mow. One word from the appraisers, against all preferences or prayers, was enough to sunder all the ties of friendship and affection."

Fortunately, in this case, the appraisers made decisions based on some consideration of the feelings of the people who stood waiting for a judgment. Insofar as possible, they avoided separating family members. Executing what they knew to be their duty, they assigned a value to the people who had belonged to Aaron Anthony. Altogether, they were appraised at twenty-eight hundred dollars.

Frederick's grandmother, brother Perry, and aunt Betty and her children went to Andrew Anthony. Cousin Henny—who, as a result of burns, was handicapped—and cousin Tom became the property of Thomas Auld. Frederick, too, became Auld's property, but Auld told him that he could return to Baltimore to continue living with his brother Hugh.

"I was just one month absent from Baltimore before the matter was decided; and the time really seemed full six months."

5

TALL OAKS FROM LITTLE ACORNS GROW

SAILING BACK to Baltimore, Frederick must have felt a great weight lifted from his shoulders, but, though he was only nine, his years at the Lloyd plantation and his recent weeks at Holme Hill Farm had swept away all the innocence of childhood. He knew that illiteracy was a dark and hopeless state. His brother Perry lived in such a state, as did his sister Sarah—who, in a year or so, would be sold to a Mississippi planter. He knew that in knowledge lay the key to freedom.

One night, shortly after he returned to Baltimore, Frederick dozed off on a hearth rug, close to where Sophia Auld was sitting at a table, writing. Hugh Auld was away, and Tommy and his two baby brothers—born in quick succession in the years that followed Frederick's move to Baltimore—were asleep. As Frederick slowly regained consciousness, he heard Sophia reading from the Holy Bible, from the Book of Job. Frederick had never heard Job's story, didn't know that it related to the question of why, so often, good people suffered and the wicked flourished.

In a voice that Frederick thought was "mellow, loud, and sweet," Sophia read a verse of Job's lament:

Are not my days few? Cease then, and let
    me alone, that I may take comfort a little,
Before I go whence I shall not return, even
    to the land of darkness and the shadow of death.

Frederick was enchanted by the beauty of the words Sophia read. After she had said good night and gone to bed, he climbed the ladder to his attic room. As he lay on his mattress, staring up at the rafters, a previously unimagined life seemed to open up to him, a life in which poetry and wisdom might be found in the pages of a book.

In the morning, he began to talk to Miss Sophia about what she had read aloud the night before. "Having no fear of my kind mistress . . . I frankly asked her to teach me to read; and, without hesitation, the dear woman began the task, and very soon, by her assistance, I was master of the alphabet." He learned to spell and pronounce words that he had never seen before. He learned to build sentences. "My mistress seemed almost as proud of my progress as if I had been her own child, and supposing that her husband would be as well pleased, she made no secret of what she was doing for me."

When Hugh Auld learned about Sophia's teaching, he cursed mightily and told her that an educated slave was a bad slave. In a voice of doom, he said, "If you give a nigger an inch he will take an ell."* Education, Auld suggested, would make Frederick uppity. "If you teach him how to read, he'll want to know how to write, and this accomplished, he'll be running away with himself."

In time, her husband's meanness would twist and warp Sophia's natural

---

*An ell equaled forty-five inches. It was at first defined as the measure of a generous forearm.

goodness. Its immediate effect on her was to make her wish that she had never started teaching Frederick. But instead of giving way to disappointment, Frederick reasoned that if an educated slave was a bad slave, then he would learn to read and write as soon as possible.

He passed his days running errands for the Aulds and taking care of their children. He was eating heartily and grew stronger every day. In the streets, he was teased because he was a country boy, but he made friends, both black and white, and was not oppressed by racial differences. As a man, he remembered how it had been to be a black child in Fells Point. He and other black children weren't "objected to by our white playmates on account of color." Black children were at least as popular as white ones. "We could run as fast, jump as far, throw the ball as direct and true, and catch it with as much dexterity and skill as the white boys."

As the next several years went by, Frederick led a rough but tolerably happy life in the noisy streets around the waterfront. While his friend and "brother" Tommy Auld was in school, Frederick went to work in the Auld & Harrison shipyard, where Hugh Auld's small enterprise was confined to overhauling and refitting shallow-draft cargo ships. In Auld's shipyard, Frederick sharpened tools and heated tar. He began to learn to use a marlinespike—a tool used to splice, manipulate, and bind hemp rope.

In the shipyard, he made use of the letters of the alphabet, taking care not to show off what his mistress had taught him. He soon learned to spell the special words used at the yard and learned the abbreviations for them. He asked a kind ship's carpenter to help him start to learn arithmetic.

In his room, he made a desk by nailing a rough plank to an empty flour barrel and began to copy out the letters and the words from a tattered Webster's spelling book. As Tommy Auld became a skillful reader and began to write short compositions, he brought home his copybooks, which his mother proudly stored in a cupboard. Careful to avoid discovery, Frederick borrowed them, one at a time, and labored over them, until he, too, began to write effective sentences. In time, he learned the uses of arithmetic and so was better educated than many of his white friends, boys and girls, who hated school and gained very little from it. He began collecting old newspapers, hiding them in nooks and crannies in his attic room, and reading them by candlelight.

The Auld family, having moved from Aliceanna Street to a larger house on Philpot Street, was exposed to sounds of traffic—to the constant clatter of the hooves of the dray horses and the rattle of the wagons. Ship's horns and piercing whistles sounded high above the hiss and murmur of the waterfront. Frederick grew accustomed to most city sounds, but sometimes, in the dead of night, lying in his attic room, he heard the clanking of the chains dragged by slaves as they were driven toward the waterfront to be put aboard a ship and taken to an auction in the South. He knew that slaves like these lived only for a life that followed death, in an imagined promised land.

The promised land wasn't good enough for Frederick, who was entering the anxious early days of an unpredictable manhood. Careful not to mention freedom, he talked to his mistress about slave pens he had seen in the back streets of Baltimore, queried her about the long nocturnal cries of people driven toward a ship that would take them to an auction in Savannah, Jacksonville, or New Orleans. Swearing him to secrecy, Sophia told him that she hated slavery as much as he did, that the slave trade was a wicked thing.

Before he lived in Baltimore, Frederick knew religion only as a rationale for the continuance of slavery. He detested people who professed a belief in Christ's admonition "Do unto others as you would have them do unto you," then read a passage in the Bible justifying cruelty, and turned around and whipped a fellow human being. He had scorned the school of Dr. Isaac Cooper, on the Eastern Shore, where the children had been whipped routinely and had laughed at the verses from the Testaments because Cooper hadn't made an effort to explain them.

In Fells Point, Frederick was curious enough to attend first one church, then another, looking for a preacher he could trust. He listened to white preachers and black ministers until he found a black man named Charles Lawson. The man Douglass called "Uncle Lawson" lived in a ramshackle hut, but he had a way with words and recognized the talents of the young slave from the Eastern Shore. Later, Frederick wrote that Lawson—who was balding and had white hair—was a perfect image of Harriet Beecher Stowe's fictional Uncle Tom.*

Pencil drawing of a Maryland freedman, by an unknown artist. This man looked much as Frederick's mentor, Father Charles Lawson, was said to have looked.

*Uncle Tom's Cabin, to be published first in 1852, was a fictional account of slavery. Unfortunately, Uncle Tom has come to be thought of as the prototype of an old, compliant slave. He was, in fact, a courageous character. See page 123 for further comments on the book.

Lawson told Frederick he was destined to become a mighty preacher who would be involved in a great work. He said he must, therefore, learn and repeat the Scriptures. The old preacher and the young man read together and discussed what they had read. When Frederick argued that a slave could never do the things that Lawson believed that he could do, Lawson only nodded and advised him to have faith in God.

Out of Frederick's new perception of the world, gained from the teachings of his older friend, came tolerance for the weaknesses of humankind. Instead of blaming slaveholders for their sins, he blamed the system for corrupting people who might otherwise have been humane.

Frederick borrowed books from Lawson, but he longed to have at least one book of his own. For his work on the waterfront, Hugh Auld gave Frederick a few pennies every week. Instead of spending them on candy, he saved them. He had heard his white friends memorizing and reciting passages from a book called *The Columbian Orator,* published in 1797, and what he had heard made him want to buy and read the book. In a bookstore on Thames Street, he paid fifty pennies for a copy, took it home, and hid it with his other treasures in his room. It was his first purchase and perhaps his most important one.

The pages that affected him most profoundly contain a dialogue between a master and a slave. At first, when questioned by his master, the slave is reluctant to engage in a discussion about slavery, saying, "I am a slave. That is answer enough."

When the master points out that the slave is given comfortable living quarters and good food and is never overworked, the slave protests that no argument can justify a master's ownership of any slave.

The master says, "It is in the order of Providence that one man should become subservient to another."

The slave then argues that his master knows as well as he does "that the robber who puts a pistol to your breast may make just the same plea."

The master, who presents himself as a good man, says that he not only has made his slave's life tolerable but has promised to provide for him in his old age.

The slave then laments, "Alas! is a life like mine, torn from a country, friends, and all I held dear, and compelled to toil under the burning sun for a master, worth thinking about for old age? No: the sooner it ends, the sooner I shall obtain that relief for which my soul pants."

At last, the master says, "Suppose I were to restore you to your liberty, would you reckon that a favor?"

The slave says, "The greatest; for although it would only be undoing a wrong, I know too well how few among mankind are capable of sacrificing [self-] interest to justice."

The master then declares that the slave is a free man and the slave replies, "Now I am indeed your servant, though not your slave. And as the first return I can make for your kindness, I will tell you freely the condition in which you live. You are surrounded by implacable foes, who long for a safe opportunity to revenge upon you and the other planters all the miseries they have endured. . . . Superior force alone can give you security."

Frederick was also deeply touched by a speech by an Irish patriot Daniel O'Connell, who was campaigning against laws that prevented Catholics from serving in the British Parliament. In the speech included in the *Orator,* O'Connell said, "I here avow myself the zealous and earnest advocate for the most unqualified emancipation of my catholic countrymen. For this cause, he said, "I will risk every thing dear to me on this earth."

Frederick read and reread the *Orator,* memorizing parts of it. He came across a poem in the book said to have been written by a teacher and delivered by a boy of seven. In part, it read:

Large streams from little fountains flow;
Tall oaks from little acorns grow;

As a child, Frederick had been afraid of growing up; now he couldn't wait to realize this prophecy.

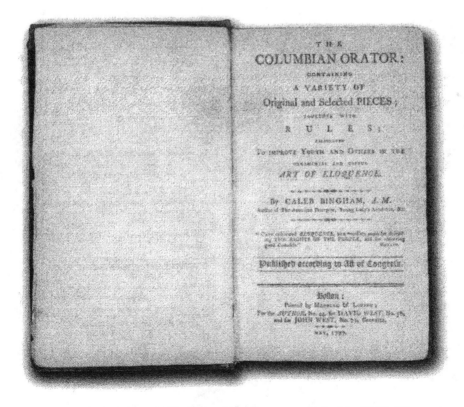

The title page of a first edition of *The Columbian Orator,* pubished in 1797. His master gave Frederick a few pennies every week and Frederick saved until he could buy a copy of the book.

In the *Baltimore American,* he found stories about abolitionists—people who were speaking out against the sin of slavery. He knew that most of them lived in the North—that fabled world where a slave might somehow win his freedom. He probably never read or heard that William Lloyd Garrison was in Baltimore in 1829, helping antislavery activist Benjamin Lundy publish a newspaper called *Genius of Universal Emancipation,* that Garrison had accused a New England merchant of illegally transporting seventy-five slaves from Baltimore to New Orleans. Later, Frederick learned the details of the case, learned that Garrison had writ-

An illustration of Nat Turner in 1831, plotting his slave insurrection.

ten truthfully but nonetheless was accused of slander, was convicted, and spent seven weeks in jail before he went back to New England.

In August 1831, momentous news reached slaveholders in America. It swept through Maryland like a tidal wave. Most slaves heard the news, even those on remote plantations in the Deep South.

In neighboring Virginia, in Southampton County, a slave named Nat Turner had planned and led an insurrection. In the misty early-morning hours of August 22, he and six other slaves crept silently toward the house where their master and the members of his family slept. They killed him and his wife and children in their beds and, joined by other slaves, went on to murder overseers and a few townspeople. By the time they were caught, they had killed fourteen men, nineteen women, and twenty-four children. In reprisal, armed white men killed almost one hundred slaves, most of whom were innocent.

Black men in Maryland were among the first to suffer in the wake of the bloodiest slave uprising in the history of America. Slave owners reasoned that if such a thing could happen in Virginia, it could happen anywhere. White Marylanders, many of them not slaveholders, cleaned their pistols and their muskets, loaded them, and set out to defend themselves. Self-appointed vigilantes roamed the streets of Baltimore, capturing and sometimes killing both slaves and free black people. A worker at the Auld & Harrison shipyard bragged that he had killed two slaves. The killer said that if other people did as he had done, the white citizens of Fells Point wouldn't have to bother with "the damned niggers."

In December 1831, also in the *Baltimore American,* Frederick read about antislavery legislator John Quincy Adams, who had been president of the United States. He had been defeated in his bid for reelection, then had taken up the duties of a congressman from his native Massachusetts.

John Quincy Adams was the son of a president of the United States and was himself president from 1825–1829. When Douglass read about him and admired him, he was serving in the U.S. House of Representatives.

Mincing no words, Adams had termed slavery "the great and foul stain upon the North American Union."

Although Frederick didn't understand the legislative process, he had read enough to know the meaning of a petition introduced by Adams in the House of Representatives. It read, "We believe slavery and the slave trade is a great national and moral evil." Adams asked his fellow congressmen to "pass such law or laws as will entirely abolish slavery and the slave trade in the District of Columbia."

In 1833, Frederick was sent back to the Eastern Shore at the request of Thomas Auld, who was still his legal owner. Some said that the brothers quarreled with each other. Thomas seems to have resented having to take care of Henny, who was so severely handicapped that she was of little use to anyone, while Hugh had the use of Frederick, who, by then, was old enough and strong enough to work effectively. Certainly, both brothers had observed a deep rebellious streak in Frederick, and both knew that it would be easier for him to make good an escape from the streets of Baltimore than from the Eastern Shore's spiderweb of slim peninsulas and marshlands.

6

THE DARK NIGHT
OF SLAVERY

FREDERICK WAS fifteen when he was sent back to Thomas Auld in St. Michaels. On an early day in spring, standing on the white pine deck of the sloop, *Amanda,* he was carried from Fells Point, out of the inner harbor, to the waters of the Chesapeake. Sailing south in the bay, he was by then determined, against heavy odds, to escape from slavery. "On my passage, I paid particular attention to the direction which the steamboats took to go to Philadelphia. I found, instead of going down . . . they went up the bay."

This was, of course, because the Chesapeake and Delaware Canal—connecting the north end of the Chesapeake Bay with the Delaware River—had been opened three years earlier, shortening the voyage north by two hundred miles or more. Frederick must have known about the new canal, but it isn't altogether clear what this knowledge meant to him. He probably realized that, living in St. Michaels, he would have little or no chance of hiding on a ship that was bound for Philadelphia. But incomplete and misleading as his knowledge may have been, he clung to the notion of escaping over water. "I resolved to wait only so long as the offering of a favorable opportunity."

After the *Amanda* sailed south in the Chesapeake, she rounded Kent Point, heading for the narrow curving channel that would take her toward the steeples of St. Michaels. As he passed the entrance to the Wye, Frederick must have thought about his "old master" Aaron Anthony, who might have been his father, and his daughter Lucretia, who had been so kind to him, had dressed his wounds, and probably had had a hand in sending him to Baltimore.

Now Frederick fully realized how hopeless were the circumstances of the other members of his family. As slaves, not only were they suffering indignity, frequent pain, and separation from their loved ones, but they had no control whatsoever over their frail destinies. Frederick, too, woke up every morning knowing that he might, at any time, find himself on an island off the coast of Georgia or entrapped in a swamp in the delta of the Mississippi. How then could he keep alive his determination to escape?

Most slave songs expressed a loss of hope for freedom in an earthbound state. Having suffered purgatory here on earth, slaves believed that after death, they would go directly to a place where they would meet God face-to-face; God would be merciful and kind.

> *O Canaan, sweet Canaan,*
> *I am bound for the land of Canaan!*

To Frederick, words like these spoke of escape to a free country here on earth—to a free state or to Canada or Britain, an escape to any land where slavery had been outlawed, and where he would find a welcome.

St. Michaels was a shipbuilding village, a much smaller version of Fells

Point. The shipyards around the harbor built small boats designed for watermen—men who dredged for oysters, gathered crabs, or dragged fishnets—and the docks were thronged with boats like these. The unpainted shacks and houses of the town, darkened by the winter storms that swept across the Chesapeake, stood beside redbrick houses owned by the proud descendants of the early colonists.

Thomas Auld had inherited the right to determine Frederick's destiny. Following Lucretia's death, Auld had married Rowena Hamilton, who shared her husband's view of slavery.

If Frederick had found Master Hugh a heartless man, he found Hugh's brother Thomas nothing short of diabolical. Thomas, something of a coward, chose not to whip the teenage Frederick, but took out his anger on his female slaves. He took special pleasure in abusing Henny, who was all but helpless. Later in his *Narrative,* Frederick wrote that Thomas Auld not only gloried in these whippings but "found religious sanction for his cruelty." He wrote, "I have seen him tie up [Henny] and whip her with heavy cowskin upon her naked shoulders, causing the warm red blood to drip; and, in justification of the bloody deed, he would quote this passage of Scripture: 'He that knoweth his master's will, and doeth it not, shall be beaten with many stripes.'

"Master would keep this lacerated young woman tied up in this horrid situation four or five hours at time. I have known him to tie her up early in the morning, and whip her before breakfast; leave her, go to his store, return at dinner, and whip her again, cutting her in the places already made raw with his cruel lash."

The only sunshine in this otherwise dismal household was provided by Amanda Auld, daughter of Lucretia. Frederick saw her mother's kindness "shining in the face of little Amanda."

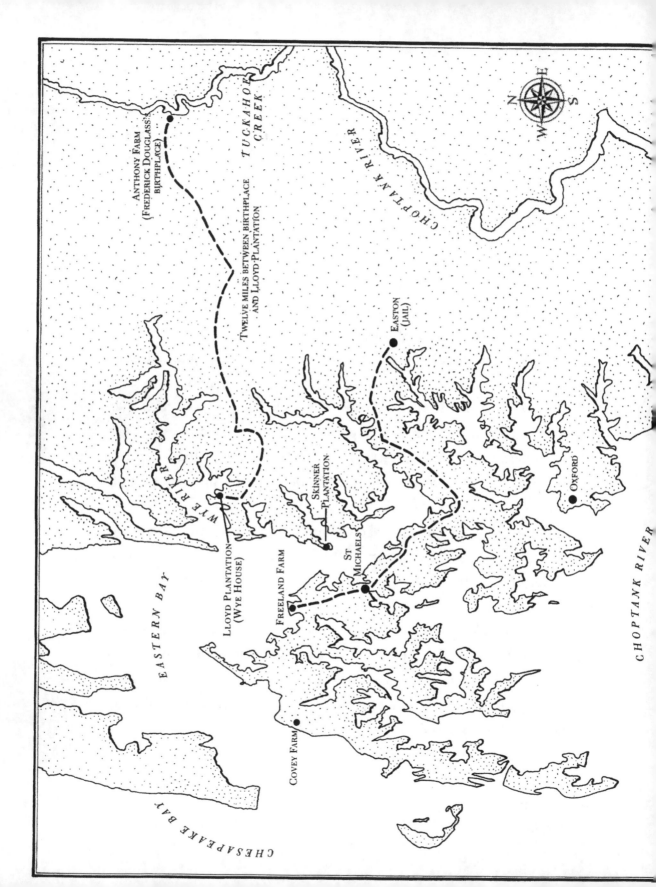

• • •

Not long after his arrival in St. Michaels, Frederick met a cultivated Englishman named George Cookman, who, it was said, had persuaded at least one slaveholder to release his slaves. Cookman coaxed "a white young man, a Mr. Wilson . . . to keep a Sabbath school for the instruction of such slaves as might be disposed to learn to read the New Testament."

Wilson dug out several copies of the Holy Bible and some spelling books and went about encouraging twenty people, mostly children, to meet in a spacious cabin built by a black man who had somehow gained his freedom. Frederick volunteered to become a teacher in the school, thus revealing to his master that he had acquired an education.

Under a law passed by colonists one hundred years before, local constables could break up "tumultuous meetings of slaves," but there was no law preventing anyone from teaching slaves to read the Bible. In this case, custom took the upper hand. Frederick, the good Mr. Wilson, and the luckless and unlettered students were attacked by a gang of slaveholders who, with "many others, came upon us with sticks and other missiles, drove us off, and forbade us to meet again." With a dash of sarcasm, Frederick wrote, "Thus ended our little Sabbath school in the pious town of St. Michaels."

Soon after, Cookman was compelled to leave the Eastern Shore. Thomas Auld, enraged by Frederick's effort to instruct his fellow slaves, and by what he thought of as the young man's arrogance, decided that Frederick's spirit must be broken. Accordingly, he hired him out to tenant farmer Edward Covey, who was known as a tormentor of black people, a man who could break a horse and break a slave.

Covey paid Auld in advance for a year of Frederick's services, it being understood that if Frederick ran away or died, Auld would return the money. As it turned out, Covey got more than he bargained for.

Wearing only his thin city clothes against the January cold and damp, Frederick climbed into Auld's delivery wagon and was taken to meet Covey. Covey's farm, six miles from St. Michaels, was on a lovely stretch of land that overlooked the waters of the Chesapeake. Covey's fields were backed, and sometimes hemmed in, by networks of creeks and estuaries. In some places, they were bordered by thickly wooded lowland patches.

Always thinking of escape, Frederick paid close attention to the route that led to Covey's place. He saw that he would soon be living in a trap. The road between St. Michaels and the farm ran across thin necks of land, where one man, armed with a musket or a pistol, could arrest or kill a runaway.

If Frederick was comforted by the memory of Lucretia Auld, he was destined for entirely different reasons never to forget his new master. Covey was under six feet tall, "more a bull than a giraffe." His neck was short, his shoulders wide and round. He was "of thin and wolfish visage; with a pair of small greenish-gray eyes, set well back." His eyes were "constantly in motion, and floating his passions, rather than his thoughts." Frederick failed to find in him a shred of mercy. "The creature presented an appearance altogether ferocious and sinister, disagreeable and forbidding. . . . When he spoke, it was from the corner of his mouth, and in a sort of light growl, like a dog, when an attempt is made to take a bone from him."

Covey's unpainted house, humble as it was, contained not only Covey and his wife, but one of his sisters, his cousin Bill Hughes, who was in his teens, and a white cook named Caroline. Frederick slept in a dusty corner of the attic, where the cold penetrated his thin blanket and caused him to shiver constantly.

Three days after Frederick moved to Covey's house, Covey whipped him, not because he had been disobedient but as a man would begin to break an animal. "Under his heavy blows, blood flowed freely, and welts were left on my back as large as my little finger. The sores on my back, from this flogging, continued for weeks, for they were kept open by the rough and coarse cloth which I wore for shirting." This was the first of many whippings that preceded a showdown.

Frederick worked with Bill Hughes, doing winter chores, cutting and hauling wood for the potbellied stoves that warmed the house, mending broken fences, tending animals. Having spent most of his youth in Baltimore, he was at first awkward, almost clumsy. On a frigid January day, Covey ordered him to hitch a team of only partly broken oxen to a cart

and to load and pull a stack of logs from a clearing in a wood to the barnyard. He put a yoke on the oxen, but the unruly beasts rebelled and overturned and smashed the cart.

Surveying the wreckage, Covey took deliberate action. He cut and trimmed three branches from a gum tree, tore off Frederick's ragged shirt, and gave him yet another vicious whipping.

In a narrow sense, Covey was religious. He read and quoted almost constantly from the Bible. He had a tin ear and a

In this drawing from 1853 Edward Covey, the slave-breaker, whips young Douglass for letting the oxen get out of control.

51

harsh voice, but all day, day after day, he sang hymns and recited from a prayer book. As if this hypocrisy were not enough, he bought a female slave for what he said were "breeding purposes," and shut her up night after night with another slave until, at last, the hapless woman gave birth to a set of twins.

Even a strong man like Frederick could be broken. He remembered later, "I was completely wrecked, changed and bewildered; goaded almost to madness at one time, and at another reconciling myself to my wretched condition. . . . My natural elasticity was crushed; my intellect languished; the disposition to read departed; the cheerful spark that lingered about my eye died; the dark night of slavery closed in upon me."

He took no comfort from the passing traffic on the Chesapeake, "whose broad bosom was ever white with sails from every quarter of the habitable globe. Those beautiful vessels, robed in purest white, so delightful to the eye of the freemen, were to me so many shrouded ghosts, to terrify and torment me with thoughts of my wretched condition."

Sundays were days of rest, but they brought Frederick no respite. "I have often, in the deep stillness of a summer's Sabbath, stood all alone upon the banks of that noble bay, and traced, with saddened heart and tearful eye, the countless number of sails moving off to the mighty ocean." He wrote later that his overriding thought was, *I am a slave—a slave for life—a slave with no rational ground to hope for freedom.*

7

TAKE HOLD OF HIM!

ON A hot and steamy August Friday, working in a field with the hired hand, Frederick faltered, then collapsed. At first, he lay still, but then he gathered enough strength to crawl to a patch of shaded ground, near a rail fence, where he lay facedown in the mud.

Covey, who spied constantly on the men who worked for him, walked directly to the place where Frederick lay and kicked his leg. When Frederick moaned and failed to rise, Covey kicked him in the face, then walked away. Frederick gathered his remaining strength and, when Covey's back was turned, rose up, staggered off across the fields, and took cover in a wood. Although he knew that Thomas Auld would take no pity on him, he decided to return to St. Michaels, hoping Auld might want at least to protect his human property.

Traversing briar patches, wading streams, and skirting swamps, Frederick made his way toward St. Michaels. At last he reached the back door of the house where he had lived. His clothes hung in tatters, his face was swollen, and his legs, torn by thorns, were caked with blood. Auld's wife, Rowena, gave him an indifferent greeting. Henny gawked in sympathy. Young Amanda was away at school. When Auld came home, he gave no food or drink to Frederick, but did let him spend the night.

In the morning, Auld was thin-lipped and grim. He said that Frederick must walk back to Covey's farm, take whatever punishment was given him, and work until his term of service had expired—an additional four months. Later, Frederick wrote that in returning to his rightful master, he had "jumped from a sinking ship into the sea."

The long trek back to Covey's farm, along the dusty and deserted roads, gave Frederick time to think about what lay ahead. In his bruised and lacerated state, the prospect of four more months with Covey was unbearable. And what would happen to him after that? One slave in the region who had learned to read and write had been "sold South." Frederick must have wondered if his education, too, would be his undoing.

As he came within two miles or so of Covey's farm, the setting sun was reflected in the waters of the bay. As it grew dark, he went in among the trees, lay down on a scattering of leaves, and fell into a deep sleep.

He woke up when he felt someone shaking him. At first, he was frightened, then he realized that his visitor was a friend, Sandy Jenkins, who was owned by a man named William Freeland. Jenkins led him to a clearing in the wood, where a single candle burned in the window of the hut where Sandy spent his Sundays with his wife—a free woman, who worked weekdays at St. Michaels. Sandy's wife welcomed Frederick.

Frederick thought he knew the reason for the couple's kindness. "I was loved by the colored people, because *they* thought I was hated for my knowledge, and persecuted because I was feared. I was the *only* slave in that region who could read and write."

While his wife bathed Frederick's wounds, Jenkins gathered wood and lit a fire, like those that had warmed Aunt Betsey Bailey's hut long ago in

Tuckahoe. His hosts gave Frederick generous helpings of cornmeal mush and thick slices of fresh bread. At last, exhausted, he lay down on a mattress on the floor and went to sleep.

Sunday morning, after breakfast, Frederick left the cabin and went on to Covey's farm. Because Covey was religious, or believed he was, he put on his Sunday manners, greeted Frederick with exaggerated kindness, and gave him a day to rest.

But on Monday morning, Covey was a different man. Grim as death, he told Frederick to go out and feed the horses. As Frederick climbed down from the hayloft, his tormenter grabbed his ankle, pulled him to the earthen floor, took a rope, and tried to hobble him. The fall from the hayloft had stunned Frederick, but he made a quick recovery. In his exhaustion and despair, he knew that the time had come to fight or die.

Covey, sensing Frederick's change of attitude, said, "*Are you going to resist,* you scoundrel?"

Frederick, whose voice was by this time deep and resonant, replied, "Yessir."

Covey, clearly frightened at the prospect of a fight with the powerful young slave, called for help. Bill Hughes was the only other white man on the place that day, but Hughes pretended that he had no interest in the struggle. Frederick lunged at Covey, took him firmly by the throat. As Covey struck out with his fists, Frederick parried every blow. Frederick later claimed that he was "strictly on the *defensive,* preventing him from injuring me, rather than trying to injure him. I flung him on the ground several times."

The two were locked in unresolved combat when Covey called out once again to his cousin. As Hughes came toward him, Frederick went on the offensive, punching Hughes in the stomach, causing him to back away. He turned again to Covey, held him firmly in his arms, then released him.

As Covey faced the prospect of defeat, he asked Frederick if he meant to go on fighting. Frederick's voice was steady as he said that, yes, he *did* "mean to resist, come what may."

Again, Covey rushed at him. As they wrestled with each other, rolling in the dung in the barnyard, again Covey yelled at Bill to come and help. The scene here had something comic about it. Bill, who knew precisely what Covey wished him to do, affected ignorance. . . . "What shall I do, Master Covey?" asked Bill.

"Take hold of him! Take hold of him!"

Bill tossed his head as he replied, "Indeed, Master Covey, I want to go to work."

"*This is your work.* Take hold of him."

Bill walked away.

At this stage of the fight, Caroline walked by on her way to do the milking. She was tall and strong enough to help, but she ignored Covey's pleadings. Frederick remembered, "We were all in open rebellion that morning."

After a long and bitter combat, Covey, "puffing and blowing at a great rate, said, 'Now, you scoundrel, go to your work. I would not have whipped you half so hard if you had not resisted.'"

With some amusement, Frederick later wrote, "The fact was, *he had not whipped me at all.*"

The net result of the fight was that Frederick found his manhood and was never whipped again. Covey, preferring to keep his reputation as a man who knew how to break a slave, chose not to risk a beating.

WE ARE BETRAYED

O N CHRISTMAS Day in 1834, Frederick sat high on a wagon
seat with Bill Hughes. Hughes shook the reins and flicked his whip
above the rumps of a team of Covey's horses. Thus began Frederick's
journey to a nearby farm and the start of another chapter in his life, a
period during which he took a different kind of risk.

Hughes left him at the end of a long driveway leading to the small
plantation belonging to William Freeland, who owned Frederick's friend
Sandy Jenkins. The whitewashed gates that guarded Freeland's land
would soon seem to Frederick like the gates that guarded paradise. Freeland was anything but rich, but his house and its dependencies were kept
in good repair. In short, Freeland was a gentleman, in the best sense of the
word. He was kind to his people. Frederick rated him "the best master I
ever had, until I became my own master."

It was the custom on the Eastern Shore to give slaves all of Christmas
week to celebrate and, if they chose to do so, spend time with their children, mend their clothes, and make quilts and baskets they could sell to
their white neighbors.

For the first time in his life, Frederick was given liquor. "We were induced to drink, I among the rest, and when the holidays were over, we all staggered up from our filth and wallowing, took a long breath, and went away to our various fields of work."

Frederick was soon to realize that he might become addicted to strong drink. "It was about as well to be a slave to a *master* as to be a slave to *rum* and *whisky*."

He toiled from dawn to dusk in Freeland's fields, gaining strength and a reputation for intelligence and diligence. But the kindness of his new master never dimmed the vision that had taken shape in Baltimore. "Thus elevated, a little, at Freeland's, the dreams called into being by that good man, Father Lawson, began to visit me; and shoots from the tree of liberty began to put forth tender buds, and dim hopes of the future began to dawn." But Frederick was not content to sit still and let the tree of liberty bear its fruit. He had learned that only through his own exertions could he gain the freedom he longed for.

As we have seen, he knew that ships that were bound from Baltimore to Philadelphia went northeast, and he had heard that Philadelphia, at least technically, was a free city in a free state. There were slave hunters there, but there were also abolitionists in the city who helped fugitives escape to Canada.

Frederick had probably never seen a map of Maryland and so had little knowledge of the region where the slave states—Maryland and Delaware—met the free states—Pennsylvania and New Jersey. But realizing that he had no chance of escaping overland, he clung to the notion that in a rowboat, sailboat, or canoe, he could make his way to Pennsylvania. He didn't realize that even in the daytime, navigating the headwaters of the Chesapeake without a chart would be as hopeless as a journey overland. Eight miles separated the approaches of the Chesapeake and

Delaware Canal from the mouth of the Susquehanna River. Once in the Susquehanna, he would have to row or paddle sixteen miles to the Pennsylvania border. Furthermore, Pennsylvania was no promised land. Slave hunters lurked, like swarms of killer bees, on both sides of the state line.

A year after he had moved to Freeland's place, Frederick made a firm resolve to accomplish an escape before another year had passed. Secrecy was essential, so his plan unfolded slowly.

Knowing he would need the help of other slaves who lived and worked at Freeland's farm, he chose a trusted pair of brothers, John and Henry Harris, whom he described as handsome and intelligent, and another young man named Charles Roberts. Frederick confided in his sixteen-year-old cousin Henry Bailey, asking him to join the expedition. He agreed.

Then Frederick made a grave mistake. He revealed the details of his plot to his friend Sandy Jenkins. Jenkins had a heart of gold, but had every reason not to want to leave the Eastern Shore. His wife was a loving woman. He had worked most of his life for the kindest master in the neighborhood. Why should he risk everything on a plan cooked up by a youth praised by slaves and damned by masters for his brave rebellious ways? He decided not to join the expedition, but Frederick never guessed that he might betray them.

Frederick's plan was simple, much too simple to succeed. He and his fellow slaves would steal a log canoe and paddle north, following the route of steamboats bound for Philadelphia. All five of the adventurers were frightened. Frederick wrote, "Upon either side, we saw grim death assuming a variety of horrid shapes. . . . Now, we were contending with the waves . . . and were drowned. Now, we were hunted by dogs, and overtaken and torn to pieces by their merciless fangs. We were stung by scorpions— chased by wild beasts."

Frederick reasoned with his own doubts, argued with the stated fears of the four others, and continued to be optimistic. He wrote bogus passes for them all. They were to execute their plan on April 2, 1836, the night before Easter Sunday. All were in a fever of excitement in the week before the fateful night. When they knew that they would not be overheard, they sang a song:

I thought I heard them say,
There were lions in the way,
I don't expect to stay
Much longer here.

On April 2, Frederick went out to the fields to work as usual, this time with Sandy Jenkins. The Harris brothers worked close by. Frederick thought that all was ready. The canoe that they had chosen waited in a nearby cove. The conspirators had hidden flasks of water, food, and paddles in a thicket. Frederick, working close to Sandy, leaned a moment on his hoe. He gave voice to a foreboding. *"Sandy,"* he said, *"we are betrayed!"*

With what was probably a guilty look, Sandy said, "Man, that is strange; but I feel just as you do."

Soon four mounted constables galloped into Freeland's field. Roped behind them, working hard to stay on their feet, were two of the five conspirators. Frederick watched, helplessly, as they tied John Harris. Henry Harris balked at being manacled. He struck a pistol from the hand of a white man, but at last was overpowered.

Sandy Jenkins stood by as Frederick's hands were tied and he was roped beside the other men. All were forced to walk to Freeland's house.

On the way, Frederick threw the pass that he had written for himself into a fire. The others chewed and swallowed theirs. As they left the farmhouse, Freeland's wife pointed straight at Frederick. "You devil!" she screamed. "You yellow devil! It was you who put it into the heads of Henry and John to run away."

As they started toward St. Michaels, Frederick was dejected. He hoped that he and his young friends would be disciplined but not sold South. As they were dragged, barefoot, along the dusty pebbled road, Frederick whispered to Henry Harris never to reveal their plot. Harris passed the word along.

In St. Michaels, Thomas Auld became Frederick's judge and jury, but it soon became apparent that he had no proof. Faced with the threat of punishment, Frederick said, "Where is the evidence against us? We were quietly at our work."

Auld replied that he had a witness, but he was unwilling or unable to produce him. He did not pronounce a verdict or a sentence. He and Freeland asked that the five conspirators be marched on to Easton and incarcerated in the county jail until a decision was forthcoming.

Along the route of the forced march, white planters in the settlements came out to taunt the fugitives, while their field hands stole only frightened, mournful glances at them. The men suffered "every possible insult from the crowds of idle, vulgar people, who clustered around, and heartlessly made [it] the occasion for all manner of ribaldry and sport." Frederick, tall and golden as he was, became the butt of the most virulent abuse. "Some said, *I ought to be hanged,* and others, *I ought to be burnt.*" Frederick asked himself, "Where now is the God of justice and mercy?"

As he languished in the clean but damp and chilly jail in Easton, Frederick recollected every detail of the sorry episode. Who had given them away? It must have been his friend Sandy Jenkins, but he didn't want to believe it. In fact, Frederick never did condemn his friend.

A delegation of slave traders went to Easton to examine the young slaves. In rushed "a swarm of imps in human shape—the slave-traders . . . and agents of slave-traders—that gather in every country town of the state, watching for every chance to buy human flesh."

One of these rough and unsavory characters, whose breath reeked of whiskey, probed Frederick's arms and legs and poked him in the stomach. In a gruff voice, he told Frederick, "If I had you, I would cut the devil out of you pretty quick."

Two days later, Freeland visited the jail. When he appeared, Frederick thought the time had come for him to say good-bye to the best master he had ever had. Freeland had, indeed, come to Frederick's cell to say good-bye to him, but not for the reason he had feared. Speaking to him in a kind and gentle voice, he told him that Thomas Auld had decided he would take him back.

In spite of Auld's frosty, often cruel behavior, there is at least some evidence that he harbored a remote but kindly feeling for his spirited, rebellious slave. Apparently, Auld thought that the young man had done his share of suffering. He sent him back again to his brother Hugh in Baltimore.

9

ANNA

FREDERICK WAS eighteen when he returned to Baltimore. The Aulds had moved once again, this time to Fells Street.* Frederick's attic room was much like the one that he had occupied before. Although he clung, almost desperately, to his fragmentary memories of his mother and would always nurture an affection for his grandmother, he thought of Hugh Auld and his wife and children as his only family and was happy to see them.

Hugh Auld's small shipyard had failed, and he was working as a foreman in Walter Price's shipyard. He was a disappointed man and was less approachable than he had been two years before. But he did say that if Frederick gave good service, he would free him on his twenty-fifth birthday. Frederick was inclined to believe him, but he did not intend to wait another seven years to be free.

Like Frederick, Tommy Auld had put away childish things and childish thoughts, but the two men could no longer share the intense, unselfconscious friendship they had shared as children. They knew that they were man and slave, and this knowledge raised between them an impenetrable barrier.

* In later years, Fells Street became an extension of Thames Street.

Tommy had matured, but he had never suffered. He had changed only slightly. Frederick, on the other hand, was almost a different person. Bearing deep scars on his back and having risked his life in open conflict with a brutal master, he was becoming a determined man.

Hugh Auld must have been impressed, and perhaps a little frightened, by the changes in his brother's slave. Although Sophia was intimidated by her husband, she was glad that Frederick had rejoined her family. Her two younger sons, who remembered Frederick as a sort of nurse, probably regarded him with some affection and perhaps with admiration.

Auld knew that he could only profit from the management of a young and energetic slave by collecting wages for his labor, so in late April 1836, he apprenticed him to William Gardner, who was building warships for the U.S. government.

Frederick worked at Gardner's shipyard. As an apprentice, he began to learn the art of caulking—filling cracks between the planks that formed the hulls and decks of ships. Amid the pungent odors and the clatter of the waterfront, he worked with Irish immigrants and free black men.

Ireland was poor, and even though Irish emigration had by no means reached its peak, many Irish people came looking for employment in America. Although ten years later Frederick would go to Ireland and would sympathize with Irish people, in Baltimore he was faced with the stark reality of racial bigotry.

The Irish left their native country to escape starvation and disease, but, in fact, in the cities of America, Irish immigrants lived in foul-smelling tenements, and, even in the coldest weather, went outdoors to privies perched above deep slit trenches. In short, America was a disappointment to them; they were angry and were eager to improve their lot.

Most Irishmen and their sons were content to be employed as common laborers, while their wives and daughters looked for work as household servants. But because the Irish were a despised minority, they were often faced with notices that read NO IRISH NEED APPLY. They were therefore forced into bitter competition with black people for the least desirable employment.

The clipper ship *Seaman's Bride* under construction in Baltimore, probably in Fells Point, in 1851. Douglass worked in shipyards in Baltimore and later in New Bedford, Massachusetts.

Irish workers feared and hated free black people and the slaves who sometimes worked with them.

As soon as Frederick went to work at Gardner's yard, he attracted wide attention. He was tall and he was stronger than the white apprentices. In fact, one on one, he was capable of subduing any other worker in the yard.

Soon it became apparent that the Irish workers, demonstrating solidarity, had some power over Gardner, who was rushing to complete two warships by July so as not to suffer the results of breach of contract. One day, knowing that their boss was under pressure, Irish workers staged a walkout. Before they went, in a body, through the gate, they told Gardner they would not return until the free black apprentices had been fired. Gardner gave in to the demand, leaving Frederick working on the deck of a warship with four sturdy white apprentices.

If life with Covey had been hell on earth, life at Gardner's soon became unbearable. At first Frederick held his own. He ducked the first man who threatened him, then rushed at him, picked him up, and threw him overboard, where he took a soaking in the foul waters of the dock. A week later, when another man attacked him with an adze—a hatchet with a blade set at a right angle to its handle—Frederick knocked away the adze with his wooden caulker's mallet, wounding his assailant's hand and forcing him to back away. These successes frightened and enraged his enemies. The die was cast. It was clear that Frederick would soon be humbled.

One evening, armed with clubs and handspikes, the white apprentices waited in the shadows in the street outside the gate. Following the ringing of the bell that marked a change of shifts, Frederick went out to the street with his empty lunch pail in his hand. This time, it took a single surreptitious blow to topple him. Stunned, he crumpled and lay helpless on the ground. His attackers kicked and pummeled him. One kick struck him squarely in his left eye. Dimly, through his one good eye, Frederick saw several dozen other workers watching, doing nothing to protect him. One of the onlookers yelled, "Kill the nigger!"

At last, Frederick rolled free, stood up, and staggered home. He put his key into the front door and opened it. Sophia saw him reeling in. He was barely recognizable. His face was a mass of cuts and bruises. Blood was caking on his sleeves. Sophia cried out, then sobbed uncontrollably. Guessing what had happened to him, she reached out and took his hand, and as Lucretia had done years before, she bathed his wounds and bandaged them.

When Auld came home and saw Frederick, he was furious. He was fond enough of the young man to feel sorry for him, but his rage came mostly in response to his proprietary feelings. His property had been attacked and put out of service, depriving him of wages.

As soon as Frederick started to feel better, Auld took him to a magistrate, who refused to prosecute the white apprentices. No white witness to the crime came forward, and no black man, free or slave, was allowed to testify. Frederick's wounds were still apparent, and Auld argued that the judge need only look at him to confirm what had happened. But the magistrate pointed out that Frederick might well have been wounded in a fair fight, and for lack of evidence admissible in Maryland, Auld had to let the matter drop.

Frederick was fortunate in not losing his left eye. Auld was gratified that he regained his health, and he found him another job, this time at Price's yard. There, Frederick must have realized that some of the fast-sailing ships he was working on were destined to be used in the African slave trade. Three of them—the *Delorez,* the *Teayer,* and the *Eagle*—were used that way.*

*In 1820, the U.S. Congress had declared that anyone participating in the slave trade was engaged in piracy and could be hanged. But slaves were so much in demand in southern states that laws inhibiting the slave trade were ignored.

The bitter irony of his position could not have escaped Frederick's notice, but an open demonstration of his feelings was impossible, unless he was willing to accept the probability of being sold south. In any case, in later years, he never wrote or spoke about the work being done at Price's yard.

As the weeks and months went by, Frederick made many friends among black Baltimoreans, most of them free. Even on the Eastern Shore, he had tried to teach his fellow slaves to read. Now, in Baltimore, in his spare time, he was free to teach again and did so, this time with more success.

Some of Frederick's friends belonged to a debating club called the East Baltimore Mental Improvement Society. Meeting in the rooms of free black men and women, members of the club exchanged whatever useful information they could gather. Especially interesting to all of them was talk about the free states of the North. Members sometimes read aloud passages from the speeches of reformers such as William Lloyd Garrison, Benjamin Lundy, Theodore Weld, Lewis Tappan, and other antislavery zealots who had broken into print in Baltimore. They read the speeches of John Quincy Adams, delivered in the chamber of the U.S. House of Representatives. Frederick reread parts of speeches he had found in *The Columbian Orator*. He began to discover that he was a natural mimic, as well as a fluent speaker.

In a search for a sympathetic Christian service, he went to several churches in the neighborhood, but was unimpressed by the sermons of white ministers. In fact, he found many ministers not just tiresome but conspicuously hypocritical, preaching love and freedom without even mentioning a people who might never know the joys of liberty. In some of his lighter moods, he was not above imitating both the voices and the gestures of these men.

One night, after he had given an impassioned speech on slavery at the club, he clenched his fists and revealed the extent of his ambition. He declared that he would one day be a United States senator. In a time when there were no black men, not to mention any women, in Congress, this was an extraordinary declaration.

It was at a meeting of the Improvement Society, in 1837, that Frederick met Anna Murray. He was nineteen. She was twenty-four. He was a slave and she was free. Like Frederick's mother and grandmother, she was dark. She could neither read nor write and, apparently, lacked a curiosity about the world that an education would have given her the power to explore. She signed her name in a combination of block letters and childish script.

Frederick was attracted to her warm and generous nature, and she returned his affection. Because in his later writings, Frederick barely mentioned her, it is difficult to reconstruct their love affair. At first, it seemed that the two had much in common. Both were natives of the Eastern

Anna Douglass in an undated photograph. Here she is a much older, heavier woman than the twenty-four-year-old Douglass married.

Shore.* She had learned to play the violin and taught Frederick how to draw a bow and pluck a string. He had a good voice and she liked to sing with him. Both of them were so absorbed in learning songs that together they amassed a large collection of sheet music. Their love deepened and, at last, they decided they would marry.

* Anna was born in Caroline County, just across Tuckahoe Creek from Frederick's birthplace.

While she admired Frederick's energy and enterprise, Anna worried constantly about his legal status. Although Hugh Auld was his master in Fells Point, Frederick was still the property of Thomas Auld. With the death of Aaron Anthony, he had suffered through a period of cruel uncertainty. If Thomas died, he would probably remain with Hugh, but what would happen if Hugh died? Aware that Frederick lived in constant danger, Anna did what she could to reinforce his determination to escape.

1 0

ALL ABOARD!

I N 1830, the Baltimore and Ohio Railroad laid tracks along Pratt Street, close to the docks. The B&O took passengers and mail between Baltimore and Wilmington. From Wilmington, there was steamboat service north on the Delaware to Philadelphia. By the summer of 1838—when Frederick started plotting his escape—the cars of the B&O were thronged with recent immigrants, commercial travelers, and sailors.

The United States Navy and the merchant services welcomed free black sailors. This suggested a clear possibility. Why could Frederick not disguise himself as a sailor and, using forged or borrowed papers, travel north to freedom?

It was understood that he would need not just a sailor's uniform but a fair amount of money for his ticket, food, and lodging. Accordingly, Anna went to work collecting things that he would need. As she became increasingly obsessed with helping Frederick gain his freedom, she went on working as a servant for a family of rich Baltimoreans and, after hours, made a little extra money washing clothes and ironing them. She planned. She saved. She thought of little else.

While Frederick waited to escape, Hugh Auld must have sensed impatience in him. He became increasingly annoyed at Frederick's presence in his small household. The young man ate a lion's share of food. It cost almost as much to feed him as he earned, so Auld agreed to let him live in quarters of his own; pay his own rent; buy his own food, tools, and clothing. Auld would pay him one-third of what he earned. Frederick was by then a foreman, and under this arrangement, he could save a little money.

Things went well for Frederick until early August, when he started to behave as a free man, sometimes leaving Fells Point without telling Auld where he planned to go. When Auld found out about Frederick's independent ways, he realized that he might be planning to escape. He ordered him to move back to his attic room on Fells Street and, again, give him almost all his earnings, letting Frederick keep only pennies, as before.

Impatient, Frederick and Anna set a date for his departure—September 3, 1838. Their plan was peppered with uncertainties, and they were both afraid that if something went awry, they might lose each other altogether.

As they waited for the day of his escape, Frederick took pains not to let his master guess what was afoot. He reported to the shipyard early, worked long days, and gave nearly all his pay to Auld. When they could meet, he and Anna worked out details of their plan. Frederick had saved seventeen dollars. Trusting Frederick, Anna said that she would give him half of the money she had saved, keeping what she needed to sustain herself and follow him to Philadelphia or New York. She sold most of her furniture—including one of two prized feather beds. Frederick borrowed papers from a merchant seaman. Having spent years on the waterfront, he was confident that he could imitate a sailor's walk, a sailor's talk.

On the evening of September 2, a Sunday, Frederick said good night to Anna, left the clothes he planned to wear, the money they had set aside, and the borrowed papers in her room, then walked back to Hugh Auld's house.

At supper, he contained his excitement and went early to his room. As he lay down on his cot, he concentrated on the details of his plan. He knew that the ticket agent or conductor might go through his borrowed papers and discover that he didn't fit the description of the older seaman who had lent the papers to him. He planned to go to New York City, but New York seemed worlds away from Baltimore. He had been told that slave catchers lay in wait in Wilmington and even in the great free cities of the northeast.

Because Auld worked in Price's yard, as did Frederick, it isn't clear how Frederick managed to avoid detection at the start of his adventure. Auld and Frederick may have been on different shifts that day, or Auld may have taken Mondays off. In any case, as early as seemed plausible, Frederick left the house as if to go to work but went instead to Anna's room, where he changed into the ample breeches of a sailor, a red shirt, and a canvas hat. He tied a black kerchief around his neck, and pocketed the money and the papers.

Frederick had been reluctant to walk through the streets around the railroad station toting anything but a lunch pail. However, he would look more like a sailor than a runaway if he carried a seabag—stuffed with blankets and a change of clothes—through the station and on board the railroad car, so Anna had persuaded a close friend of theirs named Isaac Rolles to take a bag to the station and deliver it to Frederick just before the train departed.

Frederick left Anna at her door, climbed down a set of creaking stairs, and walked at a brisk and yet unhurried pace directly to the station.

Frightened by the ticket agent's chilly gaze, he decided not to stand in line, but to buy his ticket on the train. As he kept an eye out for his friend, he tried not to look as anxious as he was.

Rolles was nowhere to be seen when the conductor shouted, "All aboard!" In a fever of uncertainty, Frederick paced the platform, thinking he might take a chance and leave without the bag, when Rolles came, gave him the bag, wished him well, and disappeared.

As the train began to move, Frederick jumped aboard and found a seat near the center of the car. The train hissed and rattled, gaining speed. The conductor, standing forward, eyed the rows of passengers. Frederick had decided how to speak to him when the time came, but he wrote later that "the heart of no fox or deer, with hungry hounds on his trail . . . could have beaten more anxiously or noisily than did mine."

He tried not to stare at the conductor as he made his way relentlessly along the aisle, taking tickets and exchanging pleasantries with familiar passengers. When, at last, the con-

This poster, published in 1839, a year after Douglass escaped from Baltimore, gives a clear picture of the kinds of railroad trains and steamboats that took the young fugitive from Baltimore to Philadelphia on the fateful day of his escape.

ductor stood beside him, Frederick held his money in his hand. The conductor said, "I suppose you have your free papers?"

Frederick kept his voice low and steady. "I never carry my free papers to sea with me."

The conductor said, "But you have something to show that you are a free man, have you not?"

In 1838, as the British reasserted what they believed to be their right to board and search a ship that flew the Stars and Stripes, so that they could look for slaves, those Americans engaged in legal commerce were insulted by the practice and resisted. Americans were in a patriotic frame of mind. U.S. sailors were the heroes of the moment. Frederick was prepared to take advantage of this sentiment on his way to Wilmington. Looking up at the conductor as he reached for his papers, he said proudly, "Yes sir! I have a paper with the American eagle on it, that will carry me around the world!" The ruse worked. Barely glancing at the papers, the conductor, in exchange for Frederick's money, pulled out and punched a ticket, handed it to Frederick, and kept moving down the aisle. On the train, Frederick saw a carpenter he had worked with only days before at Price's yard, but the man failed to notice him.

Frederick not only had never traveled on a train but had never been away from Maryland, and he was anxious when he left the railroad car and walked with the other passengers toward a nearby ferry slip. As the ferry crossed the Susquehanna, a free black man he had known in Baltimore recognized him, greeted him, and asked him why he was dressed as a sailor. Where was he bound? When did he plan to return to Baltimore? Frederick, desperately afraid that a hostile passenger would overhear these foolish questions, mumbled answers, smiled, and walked away from his inquisitor.

Another train took Frederick on to Wilmington, where he thought he might encounter bounty hunters—men bent on catching fugitives and collecting a reward for their return—but his disguise was sufficiently convincing to protect him. From Wilmington, he took a steamer up the Delaware to Philadelphia, then a train across New Jersey.

Shortly after midnight on September 4, he rode another ferry from a dark New Jersey terminal to a slip at Fulton Street, in New York. He had by then spent most of his and Anna's money. He was hungry and so tired that he put down his seabag in a corner of a pier and slept until the light of dawn touched the steeples of the great metropolis. He spent a few coins on a modest breakfast, then explored the largest seaport in America. Here he was, "safe and sound, without loss of blood or bone . . . walking amid the hurrying throng, and gazing upon the dazzling wonders of Broadway. The dreams of my childhood and the purposes of my manhood were now fulfilled. A free state around me, and a free earth under my feet!"

On that first day, he met another fugitive from Baltimore, a man who warned him that not all black people in New York could be trusted. He told Frederick that bounty hunters watched shipyards and frequented boardinghouses where black people stayed. As Frederick heard this, his spirits plummeted. "I was without home, without friends, without work, without money." He reflected, "Some apology can easily be made for the few slaves who have, after making good their escape, turned back to slavery, preferring the actual rule of their masters, to the life of loneliness, apprehension, hunger, and anxiety, which meets them on their first arrival in a free state."

Having spent another night on a wharf, hidden among crates and barrels, Frederick walked the streets again, this time looking for someone who might be sympathetic to his plight. He found such a person, a black sailor who suggested that he visit David Ruggles, who was secretary of an anti-slavery organization: The New York Vigilance Committee. Ruggles was both merciful and kind. He gave Frederick food and lodging. Frederick,

The New York City waterfront, probably on the East River, shortly after Douglass first encountered it.

The Reverend James W. C. Pennington married Frederick and Anna on September 15, 1838. Pennington, born in 1809, had escaped in 1830 from his native Maryland.

using every possible precaution, wrote to Anna, telling her where he was and asking her to come to him as soon as possible.

On September 15, 1838, in a private ceremony, Anna and Frederick were married by the Reverend James W. C. Pennington. "A new plum colored silk dress was her wedding gown."*

Following the ceremony, Ruggles told the happy couple that New York was not a safe place for a runaway. He sent them on to New Bedford, Massachusetts, where, he said, Frederick could probably go to work in a shipyard. It was in New Bedford that Frederick took the surname Douglass.

*Anna kept her wedding gown. Years later, she showed it to Rosetta, her first child.

1 1

BECAUSE
YOU ARE BLACK

BY 1841, when Douglass traveled from New Bedford to Nantucket—where he gave his first important speech—he and Anna had
two children and a third was on the way. Rosetta was two and Lewis was a
babe in arms. In the same year, Douglass and his family moved to Lynn, a
town ten miles or so northeast of Boston, overlooking Massachusetts Bay.
They lived in a little house beside the railroad tracks.

Anna had friends in New Bedford and was sorry to lose touch with
them, but Lynn was closer to Boston, which was a hub of abolitionist
activity. In Salem, next to Lynn, lived a number of distinguished black
crusaders, including Charles Lenox Remond, a short, intense, commanding man, who for several years would work with Douglass. John Greenleaf
Whittier, soon to be known as an antislavery poet,* lived a short buggy
ride from Salem. William Lloyd Garrison lived in Boston, as did tall and
aristocratic antislavery clergyman Wendell Phillips and a host of other
antislavery men and women, most of them privileged people who had long
been calling for an end to slavery.

---

*No doubt, Douglass had read Whittier, who by 1841 was an established poet, though not yet a conspicu-
ous antislavery propagandist.

Lynn was a pleasant town, known for its promenades and sweeping views of the distant shipping lanes. Most of its residents were white, but many were progressive and had set up schools for exceptional black children. These reformers were soon to persuade their city fathers to desegregate their schools.

As it turned out, Douglass didn't spend much time in Lynn but often took a train to Boston to consult with other abolitionists. He went on speaking tours with some of them, covering New England and New York, and several western states as well.

Douglass was a loving father, but was not in any other sense a family man. With the help of several friends, he bought a horse and buggy for his wife and sent money to her when he could, but she was left to manage their household, raise their children, and work as a domestic servant, as she had in Baltimore.

Rosetta later wrote about her father's visits. "Father was Mother's honored guest. He was away from home so often that his home comings were events that she thought worthy of extra notice."

On the whole, race relations in the free states were deplorable. As had been the case in Baltimore, immigrants were competing with black people for employment—for pay that could barely feed their families. Although most free black Americans were at the bottom of the economic scale, some had raised themselves above white immigrants, becoming skilled professionals, and it was these who most infuriated recent immigrants.

Douglass knew that most white people in the North felt threatened by the possibility of a mass migration of black laborers. He wrote that they believed that "if slavery were abolished, we would all come north." He said that, of course, "we would all seek our homes and our friends but, more than all, to escape from northern prejudice, we would go south."

As Douglass traveled with his colleagues, he understood that he was in constant danger. In *The Liberator,* he had read about attacks on abolitionists. Six years earlier, Garrison had come close to being hanged on Boston Common.

On October 21, 1835, following his attendance at a meeting of the Boston Female Anti-Slavery Society, Garrison had been seized by members of a gang of young and well-dressed businessmen, probably people who bought cotton from the South, and dragged into State Street, where they taunted him, ripped his shirt off his back, and tied a rope around his waist, telling him that they meant to tar

Leading abolitionist William Lloyd Garrison was, at first, a friend of Douglass but, in time, his jealousy drove them apart.

and feather him. As they led him toward the common, several members of the mob suggested that he should be hanged. At last, he was rescued by Mayor Theodore Lyman Jr. and was kept in protective custody until his tormentors had gone home. Garrison was nonviolent and throughout his ordeal he made no effort to defend himself; even his detractors said that he had been courageous.

Douglass knew that such occurrences were common in the Northeast. He had read about race riots in New York and Philadelphia in the 1820s and 1830s. He knew about the murder of antislavery publisher Elijah P.

Lovejoy in Illinois in 1837. Garrison and Lovejoy were white men. What chance would a black man have against the fury of a racist mob?

Ignoring warnings from his colleagues and from sympathetic neighbors, Douglass went to work as an agent of the Massachusetts Anti-Slavery Society. He soon became exhibit A. Here was a fugitive from slavery, a man whose back had been scored by leather thongs. Few people in the North had ever *seen* a slave or a fugitive from slavery. Douglass was a curiosity, and in 1841, Americans had a taste for oddities. It was in that year that showman P. T. Barnum opened his American Museum in New York, in which he displayed the dwarf Tom Thumb and a set of Siamese twins. Garrison did not suggest that Douglass bare his back and show his scars,* but there was something condescending in his attitude toward the talented and fiercely independent younger man.

In Nantucket, Garrison had seen at once how useful Douglass might be—if he didn't rise too fast, if his behavior was beyond reproach, and if his speeches weren't so brilliant that his listeners would find it impossible to believe that he had been a slave and had taught himself to read and write.

Even at the beginning of their friendship, Garrison said things that irritated Douglass. Once, introducing Douglass, Garrison proclaimed that his listeners would soon be witnessing a miracle. "On this night," he said, "a chattel becomes a man." Douglass knew that despite his legal status, he had long since become a man.

Garrison gloried in the use of vivid language, reveled in his position as a leader of a just crusade. He was passionate in his opposition to his nation's greatest evil but was just as passionate in defense of his position. He must have sensed that Douglass was a threat to that position.

---

*Later, on at least one occasion, Douglass did bare his back to prove that he had, indeed, been whipped.

One of Douglass's white colleagues told him that it might be "better to have a *little* of the plantation in his speech." Garrison warned him not to sound too "learned," lest the people in his audiences not believe that he had ever been a slave. Douglass didn't laugh at his advisers, but flying in the face of warnings not to sound as intelligent and witty as, in fact, he was, he not only honed his speaking skills but further cultivated what turned out to be a razor-edged capacity for contentious interchange. He became one of the few speakers of his time who could rise above the catcalls of a hostile audience.

Douglass could never quite relax. He often took a train to Boston and in the cars encountered what were called Jim Crow laws—the segregation of black passengers from white passengers in steamboats, horsecars, and railroad trains, and their exclusion from restaurants, theaters, circuses, and museums, not to mention schools, colleges, and universities. In September, in New Hampshire, four white men dragged Douglass from a first-class railroad car, where he had been sitting with white abolitionist John Collins, who was general agent for the New England Anti-Slavery Society.

After he had many arguments with conductors on the line that took passengers between Lynn and Boston, he decided he had had enough of Jim Crow practices. The next time a conductor ordered Douglass to move to a car occupied exclusively by black people, he countered in a steady, quiet but commanding voice. "If you give me one good reason why I should, I will go willingly."

The conductor, his voice trembling with emotion, said, "Because you are black."

Douglass asked for some support from his fellow passengers, but they only turned away. He remembered later that the conductor then appealed to "half a dozen fellows of the baser sort (just such as would volunteer to take a bull-dog out of a meeting-house in time of public worship). . . . They clutched me, head, neck, and shoulders. But, in anticipation of the stretching to which I was about to be subjected, I had interwoven myself among the seats. In dragging me out, on this occasion, it must have cost the company twenty-five or thirty dollars, for I tore up seats and all."

So great was the excitement about Douglass's protests that railroad officials ordered that the train not stop in Lynn as long as Douglass lived there. "For several days the trains went dashing through Lynn without stopping." Officially Douglass was still a slave, but he referred to himself as a free man. "At the same time that they excluded a free colored man

A free black man kidnapped in New York state in the 1830s. As a fugitive, and later as a liberated slave, Douglass was in constant danger.

from the cars, this same company allowed slaves [who were with] their masters and mistresses, to ride unmolested."

In his time Douglass was regarded by most white people as a nuisance, but the kinds of protests he and others who came after him engaged in brought results. As we have seen, John Quincy Adams was an antislavery legislator. His son Charles Francis Adams, who practiced law in Massachusetts, followed in his father's footsteps. He saw to it that the Massachusetts legislature outlawed discrimination in the public railroad cars.

Most of Douglass's colleagues went with him to hotels and restaurants and walked out with him when he was told, "We don't allow niggers in here!" But Douglass found that very few of his white friends were completely without prejudice. Here were white men and women working tirelessly for abolition and for civil rights who, when push came to shove, couldn't quite measure up to their own standards. The patrician Wendell Phillips, whom Douglass called "the most aristocratic of the traveling antislavery lecturers," told his wife, supposedly in confidence, that he was uncomfortable when he had to share a room with Douglass. Another abolitionist, apparently unaware of the effect of his behavior on his black companions, sometimes told racist jokes. Twenty years later, several million people who had long been held in bondage in the South would begin to express their gratitude to these same people for their freedom, but in the 1840s, Douglass couldn't help but be aware of the inconsistencies in the behavior of his white colleagues.

On these long and lively speaking junkets, Douglass gained a brilliant reputation, but he was away from home when Anna gave birth, on March 3, 1842, to their second son, named after him. On a tour of Vermont, he gave a speech standing under a small tree, in the center of a village green.

"I began to speak in the morning to an audience of five persons, and before the close of my afternoon meeting I had before me not less than five hundred."

In 1843, on a lecture tour in New York, Indiana, Pennsylvania, and Ohio, Douglass traveled with his neighbor Charles Remond. The two men were joined from time to time by other abolitionists. In New York state, they went west on tracks that ran roughly parallel to the Erie Canal, visiting most of its major ports: Utica, Syracuse, Rochester, and Buffalo. In Rochester, they met and stayed with Quakers Isaac and Amy Post. Of the couple, Douglass wrote, "They never seemed to ask, 'What will the world say?' but walked straight forward in what seemed to them the line of duty. . . . Many a poor fugitive slave found shelter under their roof when such shelter was hard to find elsewhere."

On the lecture circuit, Douglass was soon celebrated as an entertainer who could suddenly turn serious. He was a Christian, in the best sense of the word. But he still liked to mimic sermons given by those ministers who were hypocritical enough to engage in Jim Crow practices, then, in their pulpits, preach the lessons of the Testaments.

Because his friends in Rochester—the Posts and others—were especially kind to him, and because he liked the city's tidy factories and gardens, he would eventually decide to live there.

In Indiana, Douglass had another taste of racial violence. "From Ohio we divided our forces and went into Indiana. At our first meeting, we were mobbed, and some of us had our good clothes spoiled by evil-smelling eggs."

He and his party, which included several people he had never met before, as well as Edwin Fussell, George Bradburn, and William White—with whom he had campaigned often—then went on to Pendleton, a small town northeast of Indianapolis, near the center of the state. When they were denied use of the steps outside a church and could find no auditorium, they bought some lumber and some nails and, using borrowed tools, constructed a small platform in a clearing outside town.

Word of the appearance of the abolitionists somehow reached a gang of rum-soaked racists in a nearby hamlet. These men rode into town and followed a stream of law-abiding citizens—some of them Quakers—who were going out to listen. They dismounted near the clearing, tethering their horses in a grove of spindly trees. There Douglass spotted them. "As soon as we began to speak a mob of about sixty of the roughest characters I ever looked upon ordered us, through its leaders, to 'be silent,' threatening us, if we were not, with violence."

Douglass and his friends tried to reason with the leaders, but the men only grinned and moved forward. Some destroyed the little platform; others, who were armed with clubs, started beating up the men. They "assaulted Mr. White and knocked out several of his teeth."

Seeing another of his fellow abolitionists lying helpless on the ground, bleeding from a deep head wound, Douglass picked up a stout stick. Thinking Douglass was ready to defend his associate, several of the thugs came at him from behind. One of them struck his right hand with a club, then knocked him down.

Probably afraid that they had killed him, his attackers beat a swift retreat, with some sympathizers at their heels, leaving Douglass with his "right hand broken, and in a state of unconsciousness."

Some of the Quakers in the audience came to help the fallen warriors. Years later, Douglass wrote, "I was soon raised up and revived by Neal

Hardy, a kind-hearted member of the Society of Friends, and carried by him in his wagon about three miles in the country to his home, where I was tenderly nursed and bandaged by good Mrs. Hardy till I was again on my feet; but, as the bones broken were not properly set, my hand has never recovered its natural strength and dexterity."

Later, he expressed no bitterness toward his attackers, but praised the unswerving loyalty of his friends. He wrote to White, "I shall never forget how like two very brothers we were ready to dare, do, and even die for each other."

To frustrate those who doubted that he had, in fact, been a slave, Douglass made a brave decision. He decided he would write and publish a memoir, in which he would tell the story of his childhood and his youth, but not reveal his slave name or the names of people who had helped him escape.

Narrative of the Life of Frederick Douglass, an American Slave, published first in 1845, was a telling argument against the sin of slavery. Its success was a sign that the force and volume of his work would soon overshadow the accomplishments of the poet Phillis Wheatley, the first important black literary figure in America.*

In any case, the popularity of Douglass's first memoir made him so conspicuous that he was forced to leave his native land, where he might at any time be captured and returned to slavery. He chose to go to England.

---

*Phillis Wheatley was born in Africa, probably in 1753. She was captured when she was a child of seven, transported to New England, and sold in Boston to the wife of a successful tailor. Her mistress was the soul of kindness. Recognizing how intelligent her servant was, she began to educate her. After sixteen months of study, Wheatley was speaking English fluently, reading the King James Version of the Holy Bible, and beginning to read Latin classics. In her teens, she started writing poetry, and when she was twenty-one, she published a collection of her poetry, first in England, then in America.

1 2

THE GREAT FAMILY
OF MAN

IN BOSTON, on August 15, 1845, Douglass went aboard the British steam packet *Cambria*, one of nine Cunard Line ships providing passage twice a month to Liverpool from both Boston and New York.

Douglass walked up the gangplank with his friend and neighbor James N. Buffam, an earnest, pink-cheeked man who was a loyal abolitionist. Also aboard the *Cambria* was the Hutchinson Family, a vocal quartet from New Hampshire, "the sweet singers of anti-slavery."

Buffam had tried to book a double first-class stateroom, but the shipping agent had decided that a black man couldn't travel with white passengers. Later, Douglass wrote, "American

Painting of a Cunard Line ship of similar design and the same period as the *Cambria,* on which Douglass sailed to and from Liverpool.

prejudice . . . triumphed over British liberality and civilization. . . . The insult was keenly felt by my white friends, but to me, it was common, expected, and therefore, a thing of no great consequence."

Douglass was to sleep in steerage, on a modest canvas berth. He stood with Buffam on the main deck as the ship left the dock, crossed the harbor and the bay, and responded to the motion of the sea. Although he had helped build many ships, he had never crossed an ocean; and his heartbeat must have quickened as the ship got underway.

At sea, he discovered that "one part of the ship was about as free to me as another." Accordingly, he visited the upper decks, where he often walked alone, feeling freer than he ever had before. He said, "You cannot write the bloody laws of slavery on those restless billows. The ocean, if not the land, is free."

Sometimes he walked the decks with Buffam, and when spray swept across the rails, they retreated to the second-class saloon, where they talked with the Hutchinsons and with other passengers who weren't afraid to fraternize with a black man.

After stopping off in Halifax, Nova Scotia, the ship headed into the vast trackless wastes of the North Atlantic Ocean. Things went well until the day before they were due to dock in Liverpool. Captain Judkins, master of the *Cambria,* was a strong, determined, and broad-minded man. He had talked with Douglass often and had asked him about his history, as had other passengers, especially British subjects, most of whom had long since recognized that slavery was a crime against humanity.

On the final day of passage, the sky was blue and the sea flat. Judkins reckoned it a perfect time to make a point of inviting Douglass to give an informal lecture to those people who might want to hear about his years in slavery. A crowd gathered on the second deck. Among those present was a group of men from the Deep South, some of whom had been drinking heavily. An Englishman, who sympathized with Douglass, wrote, "He was constantly interrupted by catcalls, and as soon as he finished a sentence, several slaveholders would call out, 'That's a lie!' When he offered to present documentary evidence of the cruelty of slavery, they rushed at him with clenched fists."

Douglass reported that a man from New Orleans—backed by other southerners—threatened to pick him up and throw him overboard. This was a threat that Douglass thought might well have been carried out had not Captain Judkins faced up to the man and knocked him down. The event was reported in the English papers, heralding the arrival of a black man whose name was already known in England and in Ireland. Douglass wrote to Garrison, "It was decidedly the most daring and disgraceful . . . exhibition of depravity I ever witnessed, North or South."

The ship docked in Liverpool—a vast city built around its natural waterways and broad canals, all lined with docks, warehouses, and brick tenements. From Liverpool, Douglass and Buffam crossed the Irish Sea to visit Dublin, where Douglass planned to start a lecture tour.*

Dublin—on Dublin Bay, at the mouth of the Liffey—was a thriving seaport, but, as noted earlier, Ireland was poor, and was growing more so every day. Above the dingy buildings on the riverfront, a yellow haze was invaded by tall columns of black smoke. On the wharves, the stevedores wore threadbare caps and when they smiled, they displayed wide gaps between their teeth. Children, most of them as pale as parchment, with blue eyes and bony cheeks, stood in clusters on street corners.

---

*Buffam traveled with Douglass in Ireland, England, and Scotland. It must be said that in Douglass's memoirs he sometimes wrote as if he were traveling alone, when he was not. He fails to account for Buffam's movements after their sojourn in Scotland, though Buffam does appear again in recollections later in America.

Dublin's Sackville Street, as it was when Douglass knew it. It was later named O'Connell Street, for Daniel O'Connell. Douglass saw O'Connell, followed by a multitude of children, as he walked in Sackville Street. He wrote that the Irish leader, who had just come back to Dublin after a long absence, looked "at the ragged and shoeless crowd with the kindly air of a loving parent returning to his gleeful children."

We know that as a boy in Baltimore, in his treasured copy of *The Columbian Orator,* Douglass had found a speech by Irish patriot Daniel O'Connell. With no knowledge of the history of the Irish people or, in particular, the struggle of the Irish Catholics to free themselves from British rule, the young slave could not have understood O'Connell's speech, but the force and beauty of its language had stirred in him a desire to emulate the distinguished Irishman.

By the time Douglass walked the streets of Dublin, O'Connell had been jailed as a public nuisance and had lost most of his power to much younger Irishmen who were advocating use of violence. But Douglass felt it a great honor to be near him and looked forward to a chance to hear him speak and, he hoped, to meet and talk with him.

In Ireland, Douglass spoke often and effectively about slavery in America, and addressed himself to other causes, too. He preached in favor of home rule for Ireland and spoke against excessive use of alcohol, which was causing much unhappiness among the working classes. He met and talked with Father Matthew Theobald, the undisputed leader of the temperance movement. Theobald was eloquent enough to make Douglass take a pledge of abstinence. This pledge, it must be said, wasn't difficult to honor; as we have seen, in his teens, Douglass had tried and rejected alcohol.

Douglass met O'Connell toward the end of September, in Conciliation Hall in Dublin. O'Connell was then in his early seventies. Tall and broad-shouldered, he was still a vivid personality. Douglass was surprised to see how tired he looked, but when he spoke, the Irishman was as eloquent as ever he had been. Douglass remembered later, "Until I heard this man I had thought that the story of his oratory and power were greatly exaggerated. I did not see how a man could speak to twenty or thirty thousand people at one time and be heard by any considerable portion of them, but the mystery was solved when I saw his ample person and heard his musical voice. His eloquence came down upon the vast assembly like a summer thunder-shower upon a dusty road. He could at will stir the multitude to a tempest of wrath or reduce it to the silence with which a mother leaves the cradle-side of her sleeping babe."

O'Connell was to live a scant two years after Douglass met him, but even in the months remaining to him, when he walked the streets of

Dublin, he was followed by a horde of children who called after him, "There goes Dan. There goes Dan!"

In later years, remembering the great man, Douglass wrote, "No transatlantic statesman bore a testimony more marked and telling against the crime and curse of slavery than did Daniel O'Connell."

As Douglass paced the afterdeck of the ferry that took him away from Dublin and back across the Irish Sea, his heart was filled with sadness and with pride—sadness because by then he understood the tragedy of Irish history, pride because he knew that he had touched the Irish people.

It was part and parcel of his greatness that even though he had been brutalized by Irish immigrants in Baltimore, he had learned to love the native Irish. All his life, he would carry with him memories of the eloquence of Irish leaders.

Back in England, Douglass and Buffam went by rail from Liverpool to Manchester, where Douglass continued what became a marathon lecture tour.

Irish patriot Daniel O'Connell in his middle years. Douglass idolized O'Connell.

In the reign of Queen Victoria, England was a study in contrasts. It was the center of a vast empire. Its aristocracy, which controlled much of the surface of the earth and most of the seven seas, was, for the most part, arrogant and elitist. In the cities of Great Britain, the gap between the wealthy and the poor was widening.

Those Englishmen who went out to the colonies often treated native peoples with intolerance and scorn, using them as a ready labor force. The same exploitive Englishmen who secured and maintained the colonies reaped enormous benefits from slavery in America, and therefore encouraged it. But there were, among both middle-class and aristocratic English people, many who regarded slavery as a sin. It had become illegal in Great Britain and its colonies, and Britain was engaged in fighting it on the high seas, where both American and European ships still carried captured Africans to slave markets in the West.

Manchester, Douglass knew, was England's largest textile city. Its busy thoroughfares and its brick and brownstone buildings had been blackened by the burning of the coal taken from the hills and valleys of the region. Manchester's looms depended on a flood of cotton grown in the fertile fields that stretched across America's Southland. The cotton was brought in bales across the sea to Liverpool, then to Manchester by way of the Manchester Ship Canal. This was cotton raised and picked by black men and women who had been born and, in all likelihood, would die as slaves. Douglass found it strange and wonderful that the people of this foreign city—most of whom depended on imported cotton to sustain their families—were nonetheless capable of imagining the cruelties of slavery and could sympathize with slaves.

In Birmingham, in central England, Douglass saw a variety of industries that were to flourish for at least one hundred years. The city was alive, not just with manufacture but with social argument. Workers had begun to recognize their collective power, as some had in Baltimore and in other cities in America, and were agitating for the right to vote, the right to earn what they called "a living wage." These people recognized in Douglass someone who had suffered as they had, someone who had suffered *more*.

•   •   •

Increasingly, as he traveled, Douglass came to see himself as linked to all of humankind. Probably thinking of the working poor in Ireland and in England, he wrote to Garrison, "I cannot allow myself to be insensible to the wrongs and sufferings of any part of the great family of man."

While Douglass was in Britain, a crack appeared in his alliance with New England abolitionists. Garrison had risen up from poverty, but neither he nor most of his privileged friends had witnessed all the shame and pain of servitude. On the whole, their crusade was theoretical. The "Garrisonians," as they were called, seemed to want Douglass to serve not only as a token black, but as a token fugitive. They behaved as if Douglass, who had become a star of the first magnitude in the antislavery galaxy, might somehow threaten their entrenched position as the leaders of a just and spotless cause.

Wendell Phillips wrote to Garrison suggesting that they had better keep an eye on Douglass. Another member of the group named Maria Weston Chapman warned that because Douglass had so little money of his own, he might be corrupted by his admirers in Great Britain and lured away from what she thought of as the purity of her crusade: the nonviolent, nonpolitical, and hopeless effort to *persuade* a majority of slaveholders to see the error of their ways.

Douglass was understandably insulted by the suggestion that he was incapable of independent thought and was enraged by the notion that his loyalty might be purchased. His response was bold and unequivocal. He wrote to Chapman, "If you wish to drive me from the Anti-Slavery Society, put me under overseership and the work is done."

1 3

WHAT HAVE WE
TO DO WITH SLAVERY?

TALL, GOLDEN, and dynamic, Douglass was adored by British women, and it wasn't long before he was attacked again by New England abolitionists, this time for friendships he had started with female admirers. Garrison suggested that it might be time for him to return to Anna and his children.

Douglass crisscrossed England, Wales, and Scotland, often speaking three or more times in a single day. As he had in Ireland, he talked mostly about slavery in America, but often said that he was touched by the trials of working men and women: miners in Lancashire and factory workers whose backyards, blanketed by coal dust, nurtured not a flower nor a blade of grass.

Garrison had long been known in British antislavery circles, but Douglass's relentless speaking schedule made him a celebrity. A year after Douglass started touring Britain, curiosity and perhaps a touch of jealousy prompted Garrison to join him in his travels.

If the fracas on the *Cambria* had brought Douglass into the limelight, his battle with the Free Church of Scotland made him famous. In America, he had repeatedly mentioned economic links between churches in the free states of the North and those in slave states of the South. After he arrived in Scotland, he launched his first major criticism of a British institution. In Edinburgh, he revealed what was probably the strongest link he had found outside America between a Christian church and slavery. He pointed out a glaring wrong: The Free Church of Scotland had been taking large amounts of money from slaveholders in America, money sent to strengthen ties between southern planters and their markets in Great Britain. He charged that money made from the labor of Americans held in bondage was dispatched to Scotland to build churches and support its ministers.

Douglass suggested that the leaders of the Free Church send back the tainted money. Then, referring to American reaction to his battle with

A street in Edinburgh as it looked when Douglass first explored the city in the fall of 1845.

the church, he wrote sarcastically that his countrymen were apparently surprised "that a person . . . insignificant as myself could awaken an interest so marked in England."

The fathers of the Free Church failed to recognize a connection between slavery and the contributions of slaveholders. In pretended innocence, they asked, *"What have we to do with slavery?"*

However, other British men of God and many laymen raised their voices in support of Douglass and his antislavery colleagues, including Buffam, Garrison, and Englishman George Thompson, who, in 1834, had spoken often in America but had been declared a nuisance by then president Andrew Jackson and sent home to Britain.

The outcry against the Free Church was heard in auditoriums and churches "from Greenock to Edinburgh, and from Edinburgh to Aberdeen." The argument whipped the mostly sympathetic Scottish people into what Douglass called "a perfect furore." In the shadow of the soaring battlements and towers of Edinburgh Castle, partisans gave speeches and marched in the city's avenues holding signs that read: SEND BACK THE MONEY!

The upshot of the fracas was described by Douglass. "The Free Church held on to the blood-stained money and continued to justify itself in its position."

Douglass went repeatedly to London. London had a longer, more compelling history than had Baltimore, New York, or Boston. In London, the Thames was a sounding, pulsing artery. The broad river dominated the great city, bringing warships and commercial vessels from the outposts of the empire. On one hand, London was a backdrop for the aristocracy, and on the other, a sinkhole of poverty. In the poorest neighborhoods, robberies were epidemic, unwanted babies were deposited on doorsteps, and men took their rejected wives to market to be sold alongside coops of chickens, slaughtered pigs, and sides of beef. Beggars warmed their hands over bonfires they had built in gutters. Prostitutes accosted plump and prosperous men. Murder was almost as common as starvation.

In this city of dramatic contrasts, Douglass was a curiosity in great demand. In the spring of 1846, he visited Finsbury Circus, an open space lined with brick and stucco houses occupied by artisans who lived clean and ordered lives. These were manufacturers of sophisticated instruments—clocks, compasses, sextants, and machine tools—and manufacturers of books bound in cloth and in leather. In Finsbury Chapel, Douglass spoke to a deeply sympathetic antislavery audience.

In an age when long speeches were a source of entertainment, Douglass spoke three full hours. He talked about slavery in America, saying that there were thirteen free states and fifteen slave states and that the slave states dominated Congress, not just because there was a larger number of them but because a provision of the U.S. Constitution ruled that a slave must be thought of as three-fifths of a man and therefore—even though no slave could vote—each increased the number of a slave state's representatives. Douglass explained that slave owners in America believed that the federal government had no right to interfere with state laws that permitted slavery to continue. He said it was his duty to persuade the people of his nation to promote legislation that would give the federal government the power to eliminate slavery in America. He had, however, long since given up all hope that legislators from the slave states would respond to argument.

By the time Douglass spoke in Finsbury Circus, U.S. Supreme Court Chief Justice John Marshall, who had argued for increasing powers of the federal government, had been replaced by proslavery justice Roger Taney, who believed in giving more, not less, autonomy to the states—a policy that would come close to making slavery universal in America.

Britain was already taking further steps to put an end to the slave trade by blockading ports in Africa and treating captains of slave ships as no better than outlaws. Douglass said that slavery was, indeed, an international concern. It was, as his hero John Quincy Adams had asserted, "the root of almost all the troubles of the present and fears for the future."

Douglass was fond of demonstrating graphically the horrors of the institution under which he had suffered. The slaveholder,

Douglass was an ambitious walker. As he walked in London's streets, he undoubtedly saw scenes like this one, on the Thames at Rotherhithe.

he said, must rely on "the whip, the chain, the gag, the thumbscrew, the blood-hound, the stocks," to keep his slaves in line. He said, "If a colored woman, in the defense of her own virtue, in defense of her own person, should shield herself from the brutal attacks of her tyrannical master, or make the slightest resistance, she may be killed on the spot."

In Finsbury Circus, Douglass told the story of a slave auction in which a man was separated from his wife and child. He described the husband watching helplessly as his wife was examined—pinched, prodded, stroked—and at last was purchased. "His eyes followed his wife in the distance; and he looked beseechingly, imploringly, at the man who had bought his wife." He was denied the right to take his wife's hand as he said farewell to her.

As always, it was Douglass's childhood and his youth, spent as a slave, that caused him to speak with deep emotion and with absolute authority about the institution of slavery, which was tearing at the underpinnings of a government conceived in independence and born in contemplation of the fundamental rights of humankind.

Frederick Douglass became a famous antislavery lecturer in England as well as in America.

Following his stirring speech and a lengthy question period, the chairman of the meeting raised a subject that was haunting Douglass as he thought about returning to America. The chairman said, "There is not a foot of ground in the United States where Frederick Douglass's legal owner would not have a right to seize him!"

Thinking of the danger that faced Douglass in America, several wealthy British abolitionists had offered to arrange for passage for the members of his family to Great Britain and provide them with sufficient income and a house, so that he could see them more often as he continued with his British lecture tour. But he knew that he would be much more effective in America, where slavery was becoming ever more entrenched.

With this thought in mind, he began to face the realities of his position. Since his escape from Maryland, Thomas Auld had given ownership of Douglass to his brother Hugh, who still lived in Baltimore. Hugh had stated publicly that when Douglass came back to America, he would capture him and take him back to Baltimore.

Douglass's *Narrative* had been in print twenty months. It had been read in both Europe and America by almost a million people. This made him a prime target of slaveholders, some of whom might pay a handsome price for him so that they could execute him in a public ceremony, in which case his rebellion and his death would serve as a warning to ambitious slaves to keep their place, to "behave themselves." Sophisticated southerners might realize that executing Douglass would make him a martyr to his cause, but he didn't want to gamble on the wisdom of slaveholders.

Accordingly, when English friends said that they would pay Hugh Auld for his freedom, Douglass decided to accept their offer. It is perhaps not surprising that some New England abolitionists who had been nipping at his heels criticized his decision to allow his freedom to be purchased. It would be, some said, a recognition of the legality of slavery.

Douglass became a free man on December 12, 1846, when his manumission papers were drawn up and notarized in Baltimore.

In November, Garrison had left England, and Douglass went to stay with friends in Newcastle-upon-Tyne. There he met Julia Griffiths, a young Englishwoman who found him so attractive that two years after he left England, she pursued him to America and helped him fund and edit a newspaper.

On March 30, 1847, Douglass was honored at a farewell ceremony at the London Tavern. The evening gathering was attended by many of the luminaries of Great Britain's antislavery movement, including George Thompson and several clergymen who had supported him in his criticism of the Free Church of Scotland. Most of the guests were white, but present at the gathering was an exotic man of color who was not of African descent: Rungo Bapojee, from a state in southwestern India. Among those sending letters of sincere regret was English novelist and abolitionist Charles Dickens, whose childhood had been spent in abject poverty. Dickens was then only thirty-five but was already author of *Oliver Twist, Martin Chuzzlewit,* and *A Christmas Carol.*

The distinguished company gathered in a dining room, where they were given tea and cakes and were free to smoke their pipes, but were offered no strong liquor. In this large oak-paneled room, filled with tobacco smoke and the rumble of men's voices, Douglass basked in adulation.

In the great hall, following five other speeches—four of them short and a long tribute by Thompson—Douglass stepped up to the rostrum, gripped the lectern, and surveyed his audience. Cheers filled the room, lifting his already soaring spirits. He smiled and nodded proudly, waiting for a chance to speak.

Gone were the hesitations that had dogged him in Nantucket. In the intervening years, he had talked perhaps two thousand times and had taken plenty of abuse. He was aware that there were those in Britain whose dedication to commerce had made them sympathetic to slaveholders in America. He had enemies in Britain, but that night, there were none in the London Tavern. There, he was like the captain of a ship who had sailed through many winter storms and had entered a safe harbor.

He thanked the people in the audience for their applause. He said that since slavery was so firmly woven into the vast fabric of America, he found it impossible to praise his native land. "The fact is, the whole system, the entire network of American society, is one great falsehood."

He had often talked about flaws in the United States Constitution and had joined the Garrisonians in condemning that important document, one that was the fountainhead of U.S. law. In the London Tavern, he quoted what to him was an especially odious provision:

No Person held to Service or Labour in one State, under the Laws thereof, escaping into another [state], shall, in Consequence of any Law or Regulation therein, be discharged from such Service or Labour, but shall be delivered up on Claim of the Party to whom such Service or Labour may be due.*

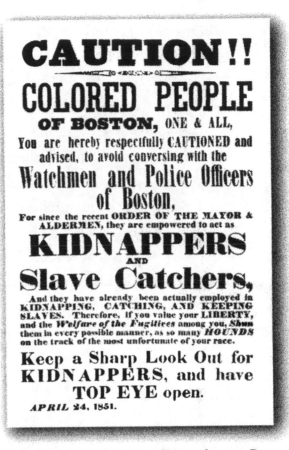

CAUTION!!
COLORED PEOPLE
OF BOSTON, ONE & ALL,
You are hereby respectfully CAUTIONED and advised, to avoid conversing with the
Watchmen and Police Officers of Boston,
For since the recent ORDER OF THE MAYOR & ALDERMEN, they are empowered to act as
KIDNAPPERS
AND
Slave Catchers,
And they have already been actually employed in KIDNAPPING, CATCHING, AND KEEPING SLAVES. Therefore, if you value your LIBERTY, and the Welfare of the Fugitives among you, Shun them in every possible manner, as so many HOUNDS on the track of the most unfortunate of your race.
Keep a Sharp Look Out for KIDNAPPERS, and have TOP EYE open.
APRIL 24, 1851.

Even living in the free state of Massachusetts, Douglass was aware of the dangers outlined in this poster, published by abolitionists in 1851.

In simple terms, this meant that a slave who escaped across state lines could be captured and returned to his or her "rightful" owner.

In the London Tavern, Douglass said that he was going home to unmask America's hypocrisy, "to denounce her high claims to civilization." His voice was deep and penetrating as he asked a question echoed

* This is a direct quotation from Article IV of the U.S. Constitution, covering interstate relations. It replaces Douglass's free quotation of the article. In 1865, this provision was repealed by the 13th Amendment.

in the next century by Martin Luther King Jr. How long, Douglass wondered, would the black people of America have to wait for justice and equality? "How long! O Lord God!"

Toward the end of his speech, Douglass said that he had been treated as an honored guest in the House of Commons and the House of Lords. Yet he remarked, in his country people thought that "the negro is something between a man and monkey."

Referring to the purchase of his freedom by his friends in England, he said, "I came a slave; I go back a free man. . . . I came here despised. . . . I go back with a reputation." Of the life and work that lay ahead of him in the country of his birth, he said, "I glory in the conflict, that I may hereafter exult in the victory."

His last words to his audience were, "With deepest gratitude, farewell."

1 4

THE NORTH STAR

ON APRIL 20, 1847, the *Cambria*, with Douglass as a passenger, sailed for Boston. From North Station, he went to Lynn, where his family waited for him in the house beside the railroad tracks.

His homecoming must have had its awkward moments. Gone nearly two years, he had changed. He was a stranger to himself and to his wife and children. Rosetta, who was eight and much taller than she had been when he left, embraced her father. His three sons, who ranged in age from three to seven, stood by to welcome him.

While Douglass had been lecturing in Britain, Anna had been learning to sew leather and had started a small cottage industry. But he expressed little interest in her work. Man and wife had grown apart.

During his long stay in England, Douglass had talked with friends and admirers about starting a newspaper of his own, and some of them, including Julia Griffiths, had promised to contribute some money to the enterprise. But Garrison and his associates opposed the project on the grounds that a string of other antislavery papers, many of them published by black people, had already failed. More than half of *The Liberator*'s readers were black. Most of these had very little money; the publication of another antislavery paper might well break *The Liberator*'s back. At least that was the argument.

It must be said that Garrison was backed not only by white abolitionists and the black working classes, but by members of the black elite and not only those who lived in Boston and its suburbs, but also those in and near New York and Philadelphia. In New York, prosperous congregations such as that of Peter Williams, rector of the oldest black Episcopal church in the U.S., helped support *The Liberator*. Black Philadelphians contributed as much to Garrison as did Bostonians. Wealthy black Philadelphia sailmaker James Forten, who as a boy had served in the Revolutionary War and had later been an enterprising businessman, had given generously to Garrison, as had his energetic daughters. Handsome and aristocratic Robert Purvis—son of the granddaughter of a South Carolina slave and an English cotton broker—had helped fund Garrison's activities.

Garrison was beholden to contributors, but was constantly on guard against challenges to his control of the New England antislavery organization and jealous of his reputation nationwide and overseas. He was an autocratic man and was capable of meanness when defending his position.

Douglass, always restless, left Lynn soon after his return from England. Momentarily convinced that he might be more effective as a speaker than as an editor and writer, he joined Garrison and others on a tour of Pennsylvania, New York, and Ohio.

On the tour of the three states, there developed further tension between Garrison and Douglass, and shortly after he returned, Douglass, with some money in his pocket sent to him by his English friends, rented office space in Rochester, New York, bought a printing press, and began publication of a weekly paper of his own called *The North Star*. Four years later, merging with another publisher, Douglass changed the name

View of Rochester, New York, in 1853, looking east. Buffalo Street, later called Main Street, runs east and west, near the center of the illustration. The Erie Canal, in the foreground, turned sharply east and ran almost parallel to Buffalo Street. The print shop, where Douglass published his newspapers, was in an undistinguished redbrick building that still stands where the main thoroughfare crosses the Genesee River. The canal crossed the river on an aqueduct. The first Douglass house, at 4 Alexander Street, stood near the far horizon.

of his weekly to *Frederick Douglass' Paper;* then, twelve years after that, he added a monthly publication, which was separate from his weeklies. Although the names and frequency of publication of his papers changed through the years, all were editorial in nature—instruments for the expression of *his* views.

Six months after he began to publish *The North Star,* Douglass moved his family from Lynn to a modest rented house in Rochester, where they lived until he could afford to buy a larger house.

Why Rochester? It was at least four hundred miles by rail from Boston and was, Douglass believed, a place where he could free himself from the scrutiny and supervision of New England abolitionists. Also, he had noted that New York State had its own reformers: men and women who were abolitionists and advocates of women's rights. In fact, in New York State, there were more energetic women activists than there were in New England. Also living in that state was the charming, vital fifty-year-old Gerrit Smith, who was prepared to give both friendship and support to Douglass.

Strategically, Rochester could become a good headquarters for the young, ambitious Douglass. It was on Lake Ontario, where there was steamboat service to the shores of Canada, making it an important stop on the Underground Railroad. The Douglass's first child, Rosetta, later wrote, "To be able to accommodate in a comfortable manner the fugitives that passed our way, father enlarged his home where a suite

This poster advertises rail and canal travel from Rochester west to Niagara Falls or east to Albany. These services were much the same when Douglass moved to Rochester in 1847.

of rooms could be made ready for those fleeing to Canada." The house was a busy refuge. "It was no unusual occurrence for mother to be called up at all hours of the night . . . to prepare supper for a hungry lot of fleeing humanity."

In 1847, Rochester was flourishing. It was at the junction of important waterways and railroad lines. Steamboats and sailing ships came north from New York City on the Hudson. At Albany, their cargo was transferred to barges built for use on the Erie Canal, completed more than twenty years before. From Albany, the barges were towed west to Amsterdam and Utica and on to Rochester, where the canal was joined by the north-flowing Genesee River. From Rochester, a bargeman could continue west to Buffalo or go south on the first section of the Genesee Valley Canal. Railroads carried passengers between Albany and Buffalo and were soon extended south through the Pennsylvania hills and mountains to New Jersey.

Not only was Rochester a good place for Douglass to begin to lead an independent life but it was beautiful as well. Large tracts of land within and just beyond the city limits were covered in fruit trees and flowers, cultivated to be shipped to distant markets in America and Europe.

At first, Douglass published *The North Star* in company with William C. Nell and Martin R. Delany. Nell was an energetic and flamboyant black Bostonian who had worked on Garrison's *Liberator*. First a journalist, he would later write ambitious histories of his people. Delany, too, was a black journalist. He had started a newspaper of his own, which had collapsed, and joined *The North Star* as midwestern correspondent. But he was something of a rolling stone and he and Douglass parted company less than a year after they began to work together.

In 1848, Douglass bought a nine-room house at 4 Alexander Street in

Water power, generated by the Genesee, together with canals and surrounding fertile lands, made Rochester an important city.

Rochester. Anna may have liked the house, but she missed her Massachusetts friends, and her husband, never one to gather dust, not only spent long hours working in his offices, but made extensive tours of his adopted state. Increasingly, he spoke out for women's rights, sharing platforms with Susan B. Anthony, Amy K. Post, and other women activists. Because Anthony and Post and Post's husband, Isaac, lived in Rochester, Douglass often traveled with them.

Although they often argued over policy, Douglass and Gerrit Smith became close friends. Douglass, at first adhering strictly to the precepts of the Garrisonians, defended strategies that were nonpolitical and nonviolent. Then, associating with New York reformers who were on the whole more radical, he increasingly regarded the New Englanders as elitist and self-righteous. More and more, he saw them as a group of people whose rigidity of vision hampered their effectiveness. He asked cogent questions. Why, he asked, shouldn't abolitionists campaign for candidates whose goals were much the same as theirs? Would only moral suasion change the minds of a people whose privileged way of life depended on slave labor? If threatened with a life of slavery, should a person not resist?

Douglass understood that no progress could be made without a monumental struggle. This struggle, he believed, must be physical as well as intellectual. Ten years later, he was to declare that "those who profess to favor freedom and yet deprecate agitation . . . want crops without plowing up the ground, they want rain without thunder and lightning. They want the ocean without the awful roar of its many waters."

In July 1848, Douglass attended the first women's rights convention, held in Seneca Falls, and spoke forcefully in support of a resolution introduced by Elizabeth Cady Stanton calling for a woman's right to vote—a right women were denied altogether or in part until the 1920s, when equal voting rights for both men and women were assured.

Douglass was a deeply loving and fiercely loyal father. In 1849, in response to overt prejudice brought to bear on nine-year-old Rosetta in her school, he faced up to her principal—Lucilla Tracy. Tracy, who was fond of Rosetta, had caved in to the wishes of the parents of the other girls, who were bitterly opposed to integration, even on a modest scale. Tracy suggested that Rosetta might be tutored in a separate room, but compromise was unacceptable to Douglass, and he initiated a campaign to desegregate the Rochester public schools, an effort that would not succeed until 1858.

In the spring of 1849, Julia Griffiths and her sister Eliza sailed from Liverpool to New York City, then traveled northwest to Rochester, taking with them a collection of antislavery literature. As suggested earlier, Julia had been strongly drawn to Douglass and the two had written to each other often. She found the memory of him irresistible.

Ostensibly, Julia Griffiths had come to Rochester to help Douglass publish his newspaper. Both Nell and Delany had long since ended their association with *The North Star* and Douglass was its sole proprietor. In spite of Gerrit Smith's contributions, he was in constant need of funds to continue its publication. The members of the Western New York Anti-Slavery Society had held festivals and fairs to raise money for the enterprise, but Douglass was no businessman and was "very hard pressed for money."

Later, Douglass was to write of Griffiths, "To no one person was I more indebted for substantial assistance than to Julia Griffiths. She came to my relief when my paper had nearly absorbed all my means, and I was heavily in debt, and when I had mortgaged my house to raise money to meet current expenses; and in a single year her energetic and effective management enabled me to extend the circulation of my paper. . . . She seemed to rise with every emergency, and her resources appeared inexhaustible."

At first, Griffiths and her sister, who appears to have been little more than a permissive chaperon, stayed in rooms in the city, but they soon moved to the house on Alexander Street, where Anna cooked, served, and took care of her newborn baby daughter, Annie. The arrival of the Griffiths sisters further lowered Anna's status and created in her an understandable resentment.

As if to try to ease his wife's distress, Douglass hired a tutor to teach her to read and write, but this only worsened what became an uncomfortable situation. Anna had a fierce, unshakable determination to remain the mistress of her home. A domestic storm was gathering.

Sometimes when Douglass traveled, Griffiths stayed in Rochester, so that she could run the paper, but most times, she and her sister accompanied Douglass. On the morning of May 7, 1850, the three traveled together to a meeting of the American Anti-Slavery Society in New York City, held in the Broadway Tabernacle.

By then Douglass was a famous man. For the time being, he and Garrison, who was chairman of the meeting, had put aside their differences. After all, following the passage of the infamous Fugitive Slave Law of 1850, decreeing that runaways could be captured and returned to their masters, they and their associates faced a common enemy. In a letter to his wife, Garrison had predicted that "our meeting [will] be a stormy one, perhaps violent in the extreme."

There were always southern visitors in New York, and some of these could not resist attending antislavery meetings. But it wasn't southerners who broke up antislavery gatherings in the city. It was northern racists.

In New York, the most powerful opponents of the abolitionists were members and supporters of Tammany Hall, a political organization long a champion of working people, at that time mostly Irish immigrants, who were always welcomed and assisted by the organization and were fiercely loyal to it. Representing Irish members was a strapping Tammany lieutenant named Isaiah Rynders, who had come to the meeting with his henchmen to make trouble.

Rynders was a nasty piece of work. He loved his fellow Irishmen, had no use for Englishmen, and hated black men. He was boss of the Sixth

Ward, which contained the Five Points district, known far and wide for its wickedness and lawlessness. Rynders was the first ward boss to hire gangsters to kill people for him. If he knew about Douglass's success in Ireland, it made not the slightest difference to him. Douglass must have known how dangerous Rynders was, but he was not afraid to bait him.

For the entertainment of the loyal abolitionists, the Hutchinson Family had come down from New Hampshire. When the quartet began to sing what Douglass called "one of their plaintive and heart-touching songs," they were silenced by "a pandemonium of hooting, groaning, and low ribaldry."

As Douglass began to talk, Rynders, who stood close to him, warned him in a loud voice, "Don't speak disrespectfully. If you do I'll knock you down."

Douglass spoke about "his enslaved and slandered people." He said, "I have the marks of the lash upon my back."

When he spoke about his heritage, Rynders said, "You are not a black man. You are only half a nigger!"

Douglass, with a faint smile on his lips, faced his audience and said, "He is correct; I am, indeed, only half a negro, a half brother to Mr. Rynders."

This riposte was rewarded with almost universal laughter, but Rynders didn't like being outwitted by a black man, especially one who had come up from slavery. Moderate politicians called on Rynders to allow the meeting to proceed and Rynders stepped aside, but he was angry and would soon exact revenge.

Before they left New York City, Douglass and the Griffiths sisters took advantage of the warm spring weather. On a balmy starlit evening, Douglass strolled arm-in-arm with his friends along the tree-lined paths and promenades of Battery Park, which commanded a breathtaking view of New York Bay and its distant harbor lights.

The Staten Island Ferry terminal—looking like a white doll house topped by a pretty cupola—was close at hand, but the visitors resisted the temptation to wait for the ferry, one of several small steamboats that crossed and recrossed the bay, connecting Brooklyn Heights, Staten Island, and several smaller islands.

In this idyllic setting, on a soft May evening, four or five thugs separated themselves from the shadows and accosted Douglass. Apparently, their language was restrained, but, ignoring the two women, they did what Rynders had told Douglass he would do if he spoke "disrespectfully." They knocked him down, kicked him almost senseless, and retired. The episode was over quickly, which suggests that the attack was deliberate and almost certainly carried out on Rynders's orders. Had Douglass been attacked on the Staten Island Ferry, he might well have been picked up, thrown overboard, and left to drown in the tide-riven waters of the bay.

From birth to death, Douglass clung to his absolute conviction that men and women of all races could both live and work together. He believed that everyone must be afforded equal rights—*an equal chance.* Some men had been his enemies, while others, such as his old friend and teacher Charles Lawson, had been steadfast friends. Women played a crucial role in forming his extraordinary character. His mother and grandmother had loved him. On the Eastern Shore, and again in Baltimore, white women had nurtured and protected him. Although some men, as Douglass said, were "true as steel," he could not resist a strong, intelligent, and loving woman—someone like Julia Griffiths. His association with such women led him to believe that "no man, however eloquent, can speak for woman as woman can speak for herself."

However this belief in the self-sufficiency of women only made him more determined to support them in their fight for what they knew to be their rights. "This is the cause of human brotherhood as well as the cause of human sisterhood, and both must rise and fall together."

During the next forty years, and beyond, he spoke out repeatedly for women's rights: the right to work for equal pay, the right to vote, the right to own and sell assets, including land. In this crusade, he augmented efforts of black women activists—women such as Ida B. Wells, Sojourner Truth, and Harriet Tubman—and befriended and worked with a host of pioneering white women.

In Rochester, at 4 Alexander Street, Douglass and Anna and their three older children engaged in what were then familiar evening entertainments. All gathered in their sparsely furnished parlor, whose walls were decorated with stern portraits: steel engravings of the leading abolitionists. There they played games of chess and checkers, put on one-act plays, and formed tableaux, which involved dressing up and posing to create a pleasant or dramatic picture. A piano stood in a corner of the room, and Rosetta sometimes sat on the piano stool and picked out a melody while Douglass and the others sang.

Alone with her family, and sometimes with the Posts and others, Anna had taken part in such social evenings, but after the arrival of the Griffiths sisters, she began to spend her evenings in her room or in the kitchen. As the tension in the household grew, Julia and her sister moved out, rented rooms again in the city, and stopped coming to the house. But their departure came too late to prevent a public scandal.

1 5

LET WOMAN
TAKE HER RIGHTS!

O N OCTOBER 24, 1850, Douglass spoke at the National Women's Rights Convention held in Brinley Hall in Worcester, Massachusetts, a small city on a hill forty miles west of Boston.

All the living pioneers of the movement gathered in the hall. These women were supported by male abolitionists who saw the need for a strong link between abolitionism and the fight of women for their natural rights. Among the speakers were Lucretia Mott, Abby K. Foster, Sojourner Truth, and Lucy Stone. Garrison was one of four men, including Douglass, who was to address the company.

On the second day of the two-day meeting, Douglass spoke with what the Boston *Chronotype* called "great force and eloquence." He suggested that the women of America become aggressive in their quest for equal rights. "You have already free access to the paths of literature; women may write books of poetry, travels, and so forth." He advised them to "strike out in other paths where they were not [then] allowed to go." He urged, "Let woman take her rights!"

Sojourner Truth was pleased with Douglass's encouragement and accelerated her campaign for civil rights. Time and again, she was expelled from streetcars, railroad cars, theaters, restaurants, and museums, as she sought to break down barriers of bigotry and prejudice.

When he was at home in Rochester, Douglass was frequently involved in the activities of the Underground Railroad. In September 1851, he and Anna helped three fugitives escape. These were men who had run away from Maryland and in Christiana, Pennsylvania, had fought with and killed their master and pursuer, Edward Gorsuch. In defiance of the Fugitive Slave Law of 1850, as well as laws against helping murderers escape, Anna welcomed the exhausted men. She set a table for them in her kitchen and gave them their first hearty meal in several days. She showed them to the narrow cots in the room set aside for fugitives and in the

Douglass often worked with Amy Post in the service of the Underground Railroad. This note reads, "My dear Mrs. Post: Please shelter this sister from the house of bondage till five o'clock— this afternoon—She will then be sent on to the land of freedom. Yours truly, Frederick."

uncertain light of dawn, cooked them a hearty breakfast, while her husband harnessed their cart horse so that he could drive them to the steamboat landing.

In 1852, Douglass moved his family from Alexander Street to a farmhouse two miles from the center of the city. That summer, in Rochester, Douglass gave what became one of his most famous speeches. It was called "What to the Slave Is the Fourth of July?"

The address, delivered on July 5, was an impassioned plea for recognition of black people, slave and free, as members of the human family. Like Garrison, Douglass had often praised the purity of Thomas Jefferson's Declaration of Independence. He reaffirmed his admiration for the document, then, addressing the white people in his audience, he asked, "Are the great principles of political freedom and of natural justice, embodied in that Declaration of Independence extended to us?" Answering the question, he continued, "The rich inheritance of justice, liberty, prosperity, and independence, bequeathed by your fathers, is shared by you, not by me. . . . The Fourth of July is *yours,* not *mine.*

"Fellow-citizens," he said, "above your national tumultuous joy, I hear the mournful wail of millions! whose chains, heavy and grievous yesterday, are, to-day, rendered more intolerable by the jubilee shouts that reach them!" Believing that slavery was becoming ever more entrenched, he said, "The character and conduct of this nation never looked blacker to me than on this Fourth of July." As he had many times before, he called slavery "the great sin and shame of America!"

Affirming the humanity of black Americans, Douglass listed all the occupations in which they excelled. He asked, "Are we then called upon to prove that we are men?" Again, he asked the question, "What to the American slave is the Fourth of July?" He added, "There is not a nation

121

White people celebrating the Fourth of July in New York in 1857. As long as slavery was practiced in America, Douglass, Garrison, and other abolitionists scorned and spoke against such celebrations. In one of his most famous speeches, Douglass asked, "What to the slave is the Fourth of July?"

on earth guilty of practices more shocking and bloody than are [those engaged by] the people of these United States, at this very hour."

Douglass's most compelling writings were his memoirs and his published speeches, but in 1853, with the help of Julia Griffiths, he wrote a short fictional account of a mutiny aboard a slave ship.* This work was over-

*This brief work of fiction appeared that year in the first of two volumes of *Autographs for Freedom,* an anthology of antislavery writings.

shadowed by the publication of another work of fiction, one that turned out to be incredibly effective antislavery propaganda. Douglass took note of the publication on March 20, 1853, of *Uncle Tom's Cabin,* by Harriet Beecher Stowe, who was soon to become a friend of his.

In Stowe's story, a slaveholder in financial difficulty is urged by a creditor to sell the child of one of his young women slaves. The slaveholder says, "The fact is, sir, I'm a humane man, and I hate to take the boy from his mother."

The creditor sympathizes, saying, "I al'ays hates these yer screechin', screamin' times. They are *mighty* onpleasant." He suggests that the slaveholder give the woman a new dress or a trinket of some kind to make up for her loss, and at last, the slaveholder says that he will sell the child.

Douglass seems not to have suffered pangs of jealousy over Stowe's conspicuous success. In fact, he wrote that *Uncle Tom* was the product of "exalted genius," calling it "the *master book* of the nineteenth century." When the book was criticized in the South, he kept his comment short and sweet: "Slavery dreads exposure."

The split between Garrison and Douglass had grown wider month by month. Originally, Douglass had backed Garrison's assertion that the Constitution was a shameful document, allowing slavery to continue. In 1853, Douglass took up Gerrit Smith's position, asserting that the Constitution was, in fact, an antislavery document. In response, Garrison said that Douglass changed his mind only because Smith had given money to him. This was a fair criticism. The Constitution, as first written and with no amendments, was, indeed, a shameful document—at least where slavery was concerned. It is hard to comprehend how Smith could have seen it otherwise, and because, on the whole, Douglass was a strong and independent thinker, it is difficult to understand why he followed Smith. But this was a question that invited carefully reasoned argument; the character of Garrison's attacks on Douglass swept away any possibility that the two men might engage in a constructive dialogue.

His justifiable position on the Constitution notwithstanding, Garrison was continuing to reveal himself as a bitter and vindictive man. He and his associates had long been aware that Douglass was adored by women. Without clear evidence of an intimate relationship between Douglass and his friend Julia Griffiths, they suggested that the two were having an affair. *The Liberator* and the *National Anti-Slavery Standard* accused him of taking money from a ruthless and ambitious Englishwoman and of letting this same woman generate "much unhappiness in his own household." Douglass was, of course, enraged at this invasion of his privacy, and he made no secret of his feelings.

In the next issue of *The Liberator,* Garrison published a short letter said to have been written by Anna Douglass. The letter stated, "It is not true that the presence of a certain person in the office of Frederick Douglass causes unhappiness in his family."

Of course, people who knew that Anna was illiterate realized that the letter was, at best, dictated under pressure. Susan B. Anthony wrote to Garrison about the matter:

Harriet Beecher Stowe
at her writing table.

We were all surprised & shocked at the appearance of Anna Douglass' letter . . . to cover all the *essentials* of the *Liberator*'s charge—for she declared to Amy Post, who happened to call there about the time, [that] it was concocted by Frederick & Julia; that she would never *sign* a paper that said, Julia had not *made her trouble*. [Anna] said, *Garrison is right*—it is Julia that has made Frederick hate all his old friends. Said [Anna], I don't care anything about her being in the *office*—but I won't have her in my house.

In view of the extended friction between Garrison and Douglass, it was, of course, ridiculous to suggest that Julia Griffiths was responsible for the breaking of already tattered bonds. In any case, an impenetrable wall now stood between two brilliant, dedicated men who were working toward a common goal.

Title page of an English edition of *Uncle Tom's Cabin,* published in 1853, the year in which it was first published in America.

Following this unsavory episode, Anna seemed aloof and proud. After all, she was not a stranger to insulting situations. Rosetta, who by then was in her teens, said later that her mother's stoicism was typical of that of "*the* black woman in American history . . . straight talking, authentic, unsentimental."

Griffiths returned to England in the fall of 1855. Whatever may have been her relationship with Douglass, she not only had helped him publish

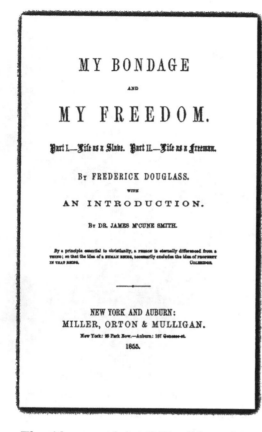

MY BONDAGE

AND

MY FREEDOM.

Part I.—Life as a Slave. Part II.—Life as a Freeman.

By FREDERICK DOUGLASS.

WITH

AN INTRODUCTION.

By DR. JAMES M'CUNE SMITH.

By a principle essential to christianity, a person is eternally differenced from a thing; so that the idea of a HUMAN BEING, necessarily excludes the idea of property IN THAT BEING.　COLERIDGE.

NEW YORK AND AUBURN:
MILLER, ORTON & MULLIGAN.
New York: 25 Park Row.—Auburn: 107 Genesee-st.
1855.

The title page of the 1855 edition of *My Bondage and My Freedom.*

his newspaper, but had worked with him on his story of the mutiny and his second, longer memoir, *My Bondage and My Freedom.*

Following passage of the Kansas-Nebraska Act in the spring of 1854—which provided that settlers in what was then Kansas Territory could decide in elections whether to be a slave state or a free one—bands of Missouri thugs, bent on spreading slavery, swarmed across the border into Kansas and attacked the barns and cabins of large numbers of dedicated antislavery settlers, most of whom had come west from New York and New England to prevent Kansas from becoming a slave state. The fight between these bitterly opposing forces was to end only with the coming of the Civil War, at which time Kansas was admitted to the Union as a free state.

On May 21, 1856, at least one hundred "Border Ruffians" attacked the town of Lawrence, taking with them a variety of weapons—swords, knives, and clubs—and two cannons. With the cannons, they destroyed the buildings of the town, including the Free State Hotel and the building that contained the newsroom and pressroom of the *Herald of Freedom.*

John Brown, captain of a Kansas settlement at Osawatomie, wasn't present at the sack of Lawrence, but afterward he declared himself an instrument of God and with a small band of men—four of his own sons and three associates—killed and butchered first three, then two more, innocent and peaceful proslavery men who owned no slaves.

The day after the destruction of the town of Lawrence, Charles Sumner—an antislavery senator from Massachusetts—was attacked and nearly killed by Representative Preston Brooks of South Carolina, in response to a speech Sumner had delivered on the floor of the Senate. In his speech, Sumner had railed against Senator Andrew Pickens Butler for his proslavery statements.

Approaching Sumner as he worked at his desk, Brooks was reported to have said, "Mr. Sumner, I have read your speech twice. It is a libel on South Carolina, and on Mr. Butler, who is a relative of mine." Brooks then repeatedly struck Sumner with a heavy cane until he lost consciousness.

Sumner's scalp was cut deeply in two places. Bleeding freely, he was carried to an empty office, given first aid, then taken to a hospital. It took him almost two years to recover. Instead of being prosecuted for his crime, Brooks became a hero in his native state. His admirers gave him a gold-headed cane.

When the news of the attack on Sumner's person reached Rochester, Douglass was both horrified and elated. In a hall in Rochester, on what he described as a "dark and stormy" night, he declared, "The time for words is past and the time for blows has come!" He

Senator Charles Sumner. The most vociferous of antislavery legislators, Sumner was beaten with a cane by a congressman from South Carolina. Sumner was a close and loyal friend of Douglass.

127

said that no peace, no just compromise, could come from Congress. Referring to himself and other abolitionists, he said, "We have the Federal Government, Executive, Judicial, and Legislative, against us."

Douglass was justified in criticizing the three branches of the federal government. President Franklin Pierce was, at best, permissive where slaveholders were concerned. The Supreme Court would soon declare itself a friend of slavery when it handed down a decision in the *Dred Scott v. Sanford* case, in which the Court ruled that black people were not and never could become full citizens and, therefore, could not seek justice in a United States court. As we have seen, Congress was controlled by proslavery legislators.

These events and conditions, together with the passage of fugitive slave laws and laws that threatened to permit the spread of slavery into western territories, were straws in an evil wind that would soon become a hurricane. By this time, Douglass knew that slavery would disappear only through violence. He had several times predicted war and when it came, would welcome it.

In 1856, an attractive and aristocratic German journalist named Ottilie Assing spent the summer touring New York State. She visited a family in Schenectady, stopped at Niagara Falls, then took her courage in her hands and went, unannounced, to Rochester to see Douglass.

Assing was no ordinary woman, and her interest in Frederick Douglass was no whim. She had read about him in both European and American newspapers. She had seen his weekly editorials, had been profoundly touched by *My Bondage and My Freedom,* and had likened Douglass to the black Haitian hero Toussaint L'Ouverture.* She had made a point of talk-

---

*Toussaint, born in 1744, was a self-educated slave. In 1791, he led a successful slave uprising, during which he defeated French and Spanish forces. In 1801, Toussaint and his generals conquered all of Hispaniola—the large island that contains both Haiti and the Dominican Republic. Through trickery, he was captured by his enemies and sent to France, where he died in 1803.

ing with the Reverend James W. C. Pennington, who had welcomed Douglass to New York after his escape from Baltimore.

On her arrival in Rochester, Assing went first to Douglass's office, where she discovered that he was at home. She might have hired a buggy to transport her to the house, but the sky was blue that day and the fruit trees were in bloom, so she walked two miles along Rochester's dusty streets to her hero's doorstep.

She knocked and Douglass welcomed her. She was in her early thirties. Half Jewish, she had often felt the sting of anti-Semitism. In spite of this and perhaps because of it, she possessed an air of confidence. In perfect though accented English, she introduced herself and told him that she was a reporter for a German jour-

Ottilie Assing. The German journalist became an intimate of Douglass. They knew each other twenty years.

nal.* Her dress, her hat, her carefully tended hair spoke to him of taste, though not of affluence. She had long looked forward to this meeting, and he must have noticed her excitement.

He invited her to come in and rest awhile. In the parlor, she and

---

*She wrote about America for *Morgenblatt für gebildete Leser*. Loosely translated, this means *Morning Journal for the Educated Reader*.

Douglass talked, as strangers do, until a woman entered, carrying a tray that held two glasses and a china pitcher. Her skin was dark. She was plump. She wore a cotton dress and a freshly laundered apron. Assing thought she was a servant, then realized that she was Anna Douglass.

Anna filled the glasses with iced lemonade, then left the room so her husband and his guest could continue what she knew was an introductory conversation. It was, in fact, the beginning of a long affair.

1 6

A STEEL TRAP

IN 1856, John Brown, whose activities in Kansas had made him and four of his sons fugitives from justice, toured New York and New England, to raise money to support what soon became a disastrous undertaking. In Rochester, Douglass welcomed Brown and took an interest in his plans. This was Douglass's first move in a direction that would put his life in danger.

Douglass had first met Brown in 1847, at one of Brown's several parched and unproductive farms—this one in Springfield, Massachusetts, on the east bank of the Connecticut River. In Springfield, Douglass recorded his impression of a man whose reputation he knew well. "He was clad in plain American woolen, shod in boots of cowhide leather, and wearing a cravat of the same

Frederick Douglass in an 1856 portrait, about the time he was in touch with John Brown.

substantial material, under six feet high, less than one hundred and fifty pounds in weight, aged about fifty*. . . straight and symmetrical as a mountain pine." His nose was like a hawk's bill. He had bright and often fierce and penetrating eyes. At that time, he was clean-shaven.

Douglass had been attracted to the man's soft voice, his capacity for tenderness in relating to the members of his family, and fascinated by the angry, violent streak in his uncertain character. In Springfield, Brown had outlined an audacious plan, a scheme that had long been brewing in his tortured and impatient consciousness. With a small band of men, both black and white, he planned to invade the South, establishing several strongholds in the Appalachian Mountains, hideouts from which he and other members of his company could sally forth and round up slaves, who, as they were joined by other slaves, would become a liberating army.

Because, in Springfield, Brown had failed to convey the details of his plan, Douglass thought it worth considering. In fact, he had himself imagined a campaign in which an army of black men, both slave and free, would liberate the several million people held in slavery in the South. Douglass left Springfield with a favorable view of both man and strategy, and during the succeeding years, he had kept track of Brown. They had written to each other often and had met several times.

In the winter of 1858, Brown showed up at the Douglass house. He told Douglass he would stay one night, but stayed two weeks. During that time he gained the affection of Douglass's younger daughter, Annie, who was then a bright and impish child of nine. He spent many hours in a spare room penning letters to his abolitionist colleagues, asking them for the money he would need to carry out his planned campaign. He appealed to many of these men, including physician Samuel G. Howe,

*Brown was then 47.

journalist Franklin Sanborn, businessman George L. Stearns, activist Thomas Wentworth Higginson, preacher Theodore Parker, and Gerrit Smith—men who were later referred to as the "Secret Six."

Brown planned to launch his campaign in the spring of 1858. But because an unscrupulous colleague ran off with a lion's share of his money and then blackmailed him—asking him for still more money in return for his silence—Brown was forced to postpone his activites.

On August 20, 1859, Douglass talked with Brown for the last time, when they and two other men met secretly in a stone quarry in Chambersburg, Pennsylvania.

Douglass went to Chambersburg with Shields Green—a fugitive from slavery who had stopped in Rochester on his way to Canada but had decided to complete a speaking tour with Douglass, then go with him to Chambersburg. The two men traveled first to Brooklyn, then to Philadelphia, and, at last, to Chambersburg to meet John Brown.

Not knowing where Brown was in Chambersburg, Douglass and Green went first to a barbershop owned and operated by a black man, who directed them to Brown's hideout. At dusk, they walked a mile or so to the quarry.

As usual, Brown was armed and on his guard. Although he expected Douglass, he and Green might have been mistaken for intruders. Standing on the knife-edged rim of the quarry—dark shapes against a luminous night sky—they were perfect targets. As Brown asked them to identify themselves, his voice echoed eerily against the canyon walls.

When Douglass spoke, Brown recognized his deep and commanding voice and welcomed him. As Green and Douglass moved toward Brown, they saw that he was not alone. Brown introduced them to a young white man named John Henry Kagi, a journalist and schoolteacher who had

This painting of John Brown was based on a photograph taken in Boston in the spring of 1859, five months before his raid on Harpers Ferry.

emigrated to America from Switzerland. Kagi had become Brown's right-hand man.

Brown had cultivated an impressive beard, but his voice and manner hadn't changed. As he talked, Douglass grew increasingly uneasy. When Brown explained that he planned to start his campaign with the capture of the U.S. arsenal at Harpers Ferry, Virginia,* Douglass frowned, arguing that even if Brown were successful in appropriating arms and ammunition at the arsenal and escaping to a hideout in the mountains, he and his guerrilla band would soon be hunted down and captured. He told Brown that he was "going into a perfect steel-trap, and that once in he would never get out alive." Douglass had risked his life many times, but he didn't want to sacrifice it in what seemed to him a vain and foolish effort. In short, he had no taste for martyrdom. However, as Brown talked about the noble purpose of his expedition, Shields Green was persuaded to join him. Douglass reported him as saying, "I b'leve I'll go wid de ole man."

Brown made a final effort to talk Douglass into joining him. With his usual intensity he said, "Come with me, Douglass. I will defend you with

*In 1859, both Harpers Ferry and Charles Town—where Brown was hanged—were in western Virginia, which became the state of West Virginia in 1863.

my life!" Such were Brown's powers of persuasion that as Douglass left him and his two recruits and began his long and lonely journey home, he could not escape the notion that he might have made a cowardly decision.

Harpers Ferry, on a peninsula at the confluence of the Potomac and the Shenandoah Rivers, contained not just a U.S. arsenal but a musket factory and an "engine house," which contained firefighting gear. It was not the easiest of targets. From the west, it could be reached over steep, sometimes precipitous mountain paths. There were, however, two practical approaches to the stronghold. From Maryland, it could be gained by crossing a long covered railroad bridge. An uncovered bridge connected Loudoun Heights, in Virginia, with the south side of the tip of the peninsula. Brown chose to approach the town from Maryland.

On October 17, 1859, Douglass was in Philadelphia. It was there that he heard about the raid, which had begun the day before. The newspaper stories were inaccurate but conveyed the impression that the raid had fallen short of Brown's expectations.

By October 19, it was clear that the raid had been an unqualified disaster. Brown and his men had reached Harpers Ferry and had stolen a few firearms. In the face of overwhelming opposition by a company of U.S. Marines commanded by Robert E. Lee—then a colonel—Brown had made a last stand in the engine house. In his attempt to occupy and hold Harpers Ferry, he had lost sixteen men killed outright, including two of his own sons. Some men who had managed to escape were recaptured. Lee had lost four men. One of Brown's men had gunned down an innocent onlooker. Brown himself was wounded. He was taken prisoner and lost no time in confessing that he had conceived and led the expedition. Six weeks later, he was hanged in Charles Town.

Drawing of the storming of the engine-house at Harpers Ferry by United States Marines, on the evening of October 17, 1859.

One of the early newspaper stories about Brown's conspiracy linked Douglass to the plot. It was clear that he was, or would soon be, a wanted man. Even so, he made a speech in Philadelphia praising Brown.

Before he left Philadelphia, he had a touching meeting with Amanda Sears, daughter of his friend and benefactor Lucretia Auld. Amanda was by then married to Philadelphian John L. Sears. Both she and Douglass may have known that there was at least an even chance that they had a common relative: his first master, Aaron Anthony.

The reunion took place in Amanda's stately home, in the presence of Amanda's husband and at least a dozen other people. Although Amanda was by then in her mid-thirties, Douglass recognized her instantly. "She bounded to me with joy in every feature, and expressed her great happiness at seeing me. All thought of slavery, color, or what might seem to belong to the dignity of her position vanished, and the meeting was as the meeting of friends long separated, yet still present in each other's memory and affection." During their long conversation, Douglass learned that Amanda had promptly freed all the slaves she had inherited.

The next morning, Douglass left Philadelphia and went straight to Newark, New Jersey, where he was met by Ottilie Assing, who took him in a carriage to Hoboken—just across the Hudson from Manhattan—where she had lived since her arrival in America. In her parlor, she showed Douglass late editions of *The New York Herald*. From the paper, Douglass learned that in a confession, Brown had named several members of the Secret Six, including Gerrit Smith. Other plotters were being sought. Virginia's governor Henry Wise had asked New York's governor Edwin D. Morgan to hand over all accused conspirators who were taking refuge in New York. Morgan was a generous and progressive man and unlikely to cooperate with Wise, but from Virginia came the news that a committee of one hundred angry southerners was offering substantial sums of money for the capture of the "criminals" who were not by then in custody. Douglass might be kidnapped anytime. Assing didn't have to tell her friend that slaveholders would like nothing better than to see him hanged alongside Brown.

Soon came the news that Douglass—who had never set foot in Virginia—had been charged with murder, robbery, and inciting "servile insurrection" in the State of Virginia.

When Assing lived in Hoboken, it was a quiet, charming town, called by one admirer "a garden of Eden." But Douglass and his friend had no time to stroll along the riverbank, as they had done before. From Hoboken, Douglass sent a telegram to his son Lewis, in Rochester, asking him to empty out the drawers and pigeonholes in his desk and destroy incriminating documents, especially letters from John Brown and Gerrit Smith.

Dangerous as it was to return to Rochester, Douglass was determined to go home again, then follow in the footsteps of the many runaways he had harbored and sent on to Canada. So as to avoid New York, he and Assing went to Paterson, New Jersey, where they said good-bye and he took a train to Rochester.

Once he arrived, Isaac and Amy Post saw to it that the coast was clear while Douglass visited his family. He loved all five of his children, but his favorite was his daughter Annie, who was described by him as "the light and life of my house."

Douglass spent several weeks lecturing in Canada before he sailed again to England. As the steamer *Scotia* left the shores of North America, he felt none of the elation that had gripped him on his first departure. "I could but feel that I was going into exile, perhaps for life."

In winter months, the North Atlantic is the roughest sea on earth and the passage was uncomfortable. Douglass noted, "Our great ship was dashed about upon the surface of the sea as though she had been the smallest 'dugout.'"

After fourteen stormy days, he "gratefully found [himself] upon the soil of Great Britain, beyond the reach of [President] Buchanan's power and Virginia's prisons. Upon reaching Liverpool, I learned that England was nearly as much alive to what had happened at Harpers Ferry as was the United States, and I was immediately called upon in different parts of the country to speak on the subject of slavery, and especially to give some account of the men who had thus flung away their lives in a desperate attempt to free the slaves. My own relation to the affair was a subject of much interest, as was the fact of my presence [in Britain] being in some sense [due to the need] to elude the demands of Governor Wise, who, having learned that I was . . . on a British steamer bound for England, publicly declared that 'could he overtake that vessel he would take me from her deck at any cost.'"

In Britain, Douglass visited his many friends, including Julia Griffiths, who by then had married clergyman H. O. Crofts. This was one of their last meetings, but the woman who had caused so much trouble in his household would remain his lifelong friend. They wrote to each other fre-

The Cunard Line steamer *Scotia*, on which Douglass sailed to England following John Brown's raid on Harpers Ferry. His crossing was at least as rough as the arrival pictured here.

quently, and much later, after she had learned about his second marriage, she penned an especially cordial letter to him, in which she said in part, "I, as one of your truest and warmest friends, hasten to send you (and Mrs. Douglass) my most sincere congratulations, and to express the hope that the steps you have now taken may tend to promote your true happiness in the evening of your days."

When his daughter Annie wrote to him, telling him about her academic triumphs, he was proud of having played a part in desegregating the Rochester public schools. But in late March, as he was about to leave for France with Ottilie Assing, he received a letter telling him that Annie had died.* Years later, he remembered, "Deeply distressed by this bereavement, and acting upon the impulse of the moment, regardless of the peril, I at once resolved to return home."

---

*The cause of Annie's death is listed as "congestion [of the] brain." Terms used then are almost useless to us now and we can only speculate about the cause of Annie's death. We do know that she was ill at least three months before she died. Douglass believed that she had died of intense anxiety about his safety and her sadness over John Brown's death.

GOD BE PRAISED!

A S HE walked the corridors and rooms of his sparsely furnished house in Rochester, Douglass must have found Annie's absence almost insupportable. At every turn, he felt her presence and remembered all her bright and loving ways. No doubt his wife grieved with him, and he may have taken solace from Rosetta's reassurances. Rosetta said that Annie was with God, "whose love is the same for the black and the white."

By this time most leading southerners recognized that one martyred abolitionist was quite enough. Although John Brown's raid on Harpers Ferry had dissolved in failure, his death had become a banner in the abolitionist crusade. It would soon inspire the words of a Union marching song often chanted on the waterways and roadways of the war that would at last bring freedom to the slave.* The plain truth was that nobody, in the North or the South, was likely to forget John Brown of Osawatomie or the cause for which he had died.

* The music was composed by William Steffe in 1852 and, following John Brown's death, became a marching song featuring the words "John Brown's body lies a-moulderin' in the grave, but his soul goes marching on." New Yorker Julia Ward Howe wrote more dignified and touching verses for the tune, which were published first in 1862 as "Battle Hymn of the Republic."

In 1860, as week followed week, Douglass reckoned that he could begin to speak again, could call attention to himself without encouraging the possibility that he might be captured in the middle of the night, torn from his family, and hustled over country roads to Virginia, to follow John Brown to the gallows.

During this period, he resumed publication of his papers, but it soon became apparent that his weekly paper was in trouble. In July, short of funds and short of time, he stopped publishing the weekly, but continued publication of *Douglass' Monthly.*

In mid-May, the Republican National Convention was held in Chicago, in a hastily constructed auditorium called the Great Wigwam. The delegates to the convention chose a tall, gaunt lawyer and politician named Abraham Lincoln as their presidential candidate. Douglass knew that Lincoln hated slavery but that he would not declare himself a downright abolitionist. He knew that Lincoln's running mate was Hannibal Hamlin, who had a solid antislavery reputation, and he knew that the most important plank in the Republican platform called for no more than a halt to the spread of slavery—a good first step but not radical enough for Douglass, who said that he was sorry "that the hosts of freedom could not have been led forth upon a higher platform, and have had inscribed upon their banners, 'Death to Slavery,' instead of 'No more Slave States.'"

Although Douglass would have liked to have had Lincoln call for immediate and unconditional abolition, still he was willing to praise him. In June, in his *Monthly,* he declared, "Mr. Lincoln is a man of unblemished private character; a lawyer, standing near the front rank of the bar of his own State, he has a cool, well-balanced head; great firmness of will; is perseveringly industrious; and one of the most frank, honest men in political life."

It was through a series of debates, most of which were taken up with slavery and the spread of slavery, that Douglass had become familiar with both Lincoln and his party's policies. In these debates, Lincoln had gone up against Stephen Douglas, a powerful and persuasive senator from Illinois, who was an apologist for slavery.

Stephen Douglas soon became one of three presidential candidates opposing Lincoln. In his *Monthly,* Frederick Douglass said that the campaign was sure to be a lively one. "If Mr. Douglas is put on the course, the old personal rivalry between him and Mr. Lincoln will render the campaign especially spicy."

In December 1860, in Boston's Tremont Temple, Douglass and a group of sympathizers were denied the right to speak when racist mobs made so much noise that nobody could be heard. The police, backed by the troublemakers, forcibly expelled the abolitionists—including Douglass—from the temple. That evening, Douglass spoke to a peaceful gathering in the Joy Street Church, which was perched on a slope of Beacon Hill. Inviting war as the only instrument capable of eliminating slavery in America, he said, "We must . . . reach the slaveholder's conscience through his fear of personal danger. We must make him feel that there is death in the air . . . all around him."

Bust of Lincoln by Max Bachmann, finished in 1905.

On December 6, 1860, in Boston's Tremont Temple, Douglass and other abolitionists tried to speak but were silenced by a racist mob. The police sided with the mob and forced the speakers to retire.

On March 4, 1861, Lincoln was inaugurated sixteenth president of the United States. In his address, delivered in the shadow of the half-completed dome of the U.S. Capitol, he continued to express a hope that war might be avoided. He noted that South Carolina had become the first state to declare its independence from the federal government. Mississippi, Florida, Alabama, Georgia, Louisiana, and Texas had since seceded, and Virginia would soon follow suit. It didn't take a military strategist to understand that if both Maryland and Virginia were to join the insurrection, Washington would be surrounded by Confederate forces and would fall. Most responsible historians concede that Lincoln had to compromise if he hoped to save the Union. In fact Lincoln was so worried that he slept and ate very little, and his face betrayed his constant indecision.

In his inaugural address, Lincoln, as was to become his habit, never even mentioned the Confederacy—the gathering of states that had already left the Union. Secession, he believed, was illegal if not traitorous; he believed that the leaders of rebellious southern states were criminals. He said, "I therefore consider that, in view of the Constitution and the laws, the Union is unbroken."

Lincoln declared that the decision in the *Dred Scott* case had been regrettable but was nonetheless enforceable. The lines in the address that most infuriated Douglass were:

> I have no purpose, directly or indirectly, to interfere with the institu-
> tion of slavery in the States where it exists. I believe I have no lawful
> right to do so, and I have no inclination to do so.

Douglass was justifiably outraged at Lincoln's assertion that he had no "inclination" to interfere with slavery. He was further angered by the president's support of fugitive slave laws—laws that encouraged capture and return of runaways. Douglass noted that the president quoted the paragraph from Article IV of the Constitution* mandating the return of slaves across state lines to their masters. He noted that Lincoln said, "All members of Congress swear their support to the whole Constitution—to this provision as much as any other."

Although Douglass couldn't argue over Lincoln's clear interpretation of the Constitution, he saw no reason why the president saw fit to emphasize this provision rather than declare his intention to encourage its repeal. In

*See page 105 for the text of this paragraph from Article IV of the U.S. Constitution.

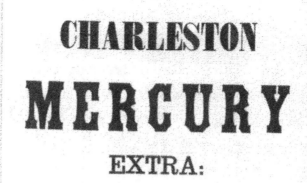

The first imprint of a broadside advertising an extra edition of the *Charleston Mercury*, proclaiming dissolution of the Union. South Carolina left the Union more than two months before Lincoln was inaugurated. Other states soon followed her example.

short, Douglass thought that Lincoln had betrayed his antislavery principles so as to mollify the South. He was therefore not impressed by Lincoln's lyrical last words: "I am loath to close. We are not enemies, but friends. . . . Though passion may have strained, it must not break our bonds of affection. The mystic chords of memory, stretching from every battlefield and patriot grave to every living heart and hearthstone all over this broad land, will yet swell the chorus of the Union when again touched, as surely they will be, by the better angels of our nature."

Not only Douglass and his fellow black crusaders, but political and military leaders in the South angrily rejected Lincoln's supplication. The time when poetic utterances might be used as instruments of peace had long since passed. Soon death would, indeed, be "in the air" in a divided and distressed America.

On April 12, 1861, Douglass was in Rochester and was probably asleep at 4 A.M. when, seven hundred miles or so from where he lived, South Carolina batteries opened fire on Fort Sumter, a federal stronghold that had long protected Charleston from invasion. The boom and crackle of the cannonade caused the people of that city to abandon their nightclothes, dress themselves, and stumble through their doorways so that they could watch the fiery demonstration.

If at first most people thought of this aggressive action as no more than an outburst in a petty quarrel, they would soon realize that the flash and sound of Charleston's guns marked the beginning of a widespread and enduring civil war, a conflict whose roots lay deep in slavery.

Later on that fateful day, after Douglass heard and read about the start of war, he spoke in Rochester's African Methodist Episcopal Zion Church. Referring to the start of war, he said, "God be praised!"

Six days after the beginning of the Civil War, he was still in Rochester when he spoke in an almost plaintive tone of the potential purity of American democracy. "But for slavery," he said, it would be a perfect system. In May, he expressed a long-held belief in a shared future for Americans. "Freedom for all, or chains for all!"

It is worth noting here that four years later Lincoln, who by then had become a deeper, wiser man, echoed this progressive sentiment when he said, "In giving freedom to the *slave,* we assure freedom to the *free*— honorable alike in what we give, and what we preserve."

From the beginning of the war, despite defeats, especially those in the East—the first of which was a humiliating loss in the first battle of Bull Run—Douglass in his writings and his speeches urged the president to issue an emancipation proclamation and enroll thousands of willing, even eager, black men in the Union Army.

Senator Charles Sumner, who had two years or so before recovered from head wounds he had suffered at the hands of Preston Brooks, was one of those few abolitionists who knew Lincoln. Sometimes after dark the two men rode together in a carriage through the muddy rutted streets of Washington so that they could talk about affairs of state. At such times, Sumner also urged the president to issue an emancipation proclamation. Lincoln was a private man; he listened but did not reveal that he was already contemplating such a move. He didn't want to talk about what seemed to him so radical a document.

In any case, in the spring of 1862, the president began to work alone on the wording of a paper that would outline a first step toward freeing the slaves in America's Southland.

While he worked, he was haunted by two monsters. One of these was a shortage of clear military victories. At the beginning of the war, he and his ranking generals had devised a strategy called the "Anaconda Plan," whose purpose was encirclement of the Confederacy. The plan projected a blockade of southern ports and control of the Mississippi River. But federal warships had found it impossible to bottle up ports and channels all the way from the southern reaches of the Chesapeake to the delta of the Mississippi, one hundred miles or so below the city of New Orleans. Fast ships, bringing arms from Bermuda, often slipped through the blockade and entered southern ports. True, the campaigns that centered on control

The bombardment of Fort Sumter, as imagined by an illustrator. Published shortly after the bombardment, the illustration shows what appears to be a dead Confederate soldier. In fact, no lives were lost on either side during the bombardment of the fort. Douglass, hearing of the start of the war, knowing that the conflict would eventually do away with slavery, said, "God be praised!"

of the Mississippi River had so far been successful. New Orleans had been captured by Admiral David Farragut and occupied by General Benjamin Butler, who, incidentally, was in favor of employing black regiments. The greatest trouble lay at Lincoln's back door, in the East, where Union armies, under General George B. McClellan, had enjoyed little or no success. In fact, McClellan was so cowardly and ineffective that Douglass thought he might be a traitor.

The second monster that hung over Lincoln as he worked on his Emancipation Proclamation was the question of what to do with the four million slaves who would eventually be freed—a people who could not at first be self-sufficient.

Lincoln had ruled that all slaves coming into Union territory be returned to their masters. He did this to pacify the border states, but, in so doing, he denied his government the use of what Douglass called the nation's "powerful black arm." In New Orleans, General Butler had ignored the president's directive and put escaped slaves—called contrabands—to work on his defenses. Butler had, in effect, instituted a contrary policy, one that endured throughout the war.

Lincoln believed that voluntary segregation was the answer to the nation's racial problems. First, he tried to encourage colonization in Monrovia in Africa, then in Panama, and on an island off the coast of Haiti. All three of these plans failed, in some cases with disastrous consequences. But Lincoln clung to the notion that black people and white people couldn't live and work with one another and should "therefore be separated."

Lincoln went every day to the War Department to read telegrams from his commanders in the field and to send out orders and suggestions. It was there, in the telegraph office, that Lincoln started writing the Emancipation Proclamation. As he worked, he spent many hours staring into space and thinking. We are told that he studied the activities of a family of large spiders in a web above his borrowed desk. He worked a full three months on the document. Still waiting for a military victory, he didn't talk to anyone about the paper.

In September, an enormous Union army, under McClellan, drove a Confederate force commanded by Robert E. Lee out of Maryland, following the indecisive battle of Antietam. McClellan's failure to deliver a decisive victory in this campaign would soon lead Lincoln to dismiss him. But the general's limited success gave Lincoln courage to release his Emancipation Proclamation. First he discussed the paper with Vice President Hannibal Hamlin, who heartily approved of it; then, at a later date, with the members of his cabinet. He promised to issue the final document on January 1, 1863.

On New Year's Day, in Boston's Tremont Temple, Douglass all but held his breath as he and other abolitionists waited for the document's release. When the news came, it was celebrated not only in New England, but was hailed by black people north and south.

In Washington, D.C., crowds of people, black and white, gathered on the White House lawn to thank and cheer the president. The Emancipation Proclamation generated deep emotion in the Sea Islands of South Carolina, where it was read aloud by a New England minister. Charlotte Forten, a young black woman who was teaching children in some of the islands occupied by Union forces, wrote that there were "crowds of lookers-on, men, women, and children, grouped in various attitudes, under the trees. The faces of all wore a happy, eager, expectant look."

The document's first important paragraph stated, "That on the first day of January, A.D. 1863, all persons held as slaves within any State or designated part of a State, the people whereof shall then be in rebellion against the United States, shall be then, thenceforward, and forever free." This paragraph changed the purpose of the Civil War. After January 1, Union soldiers, like it or not, would be fighting for the freedom of four million slaves held in bondage in the South.

The paragraph that in the short run would most affect Frederick Douglass and two of his three sons regarded the inclusion of black men in Union military services:

> And I further declare and make known, that such persons of suitable condition, will be received into the armed service of the United States to garrison forts, positions, stations, and other places, and to man vessels of all sorts in said service.

Here, at last, was a clear statement by the president of the United States of a policy that Douglass had been advocating since the firing on Fort Sumter. While nonviolent abolitionists were slow to accept the notion of a forthright military policy including black men, Douglass was jubilant, not only as he read about the freeing of slaves in states then "in rebellion against the United States," but at the welcoming of black men into military service. At New York's Cooper Institute, he said of the Emancipation Proclamation, "I hail it as the doom of Slavery in all the States. I hail it as the end of all that miserable statesmanship, which has for sixty years juggled and deceived the people, by professing to reconcile what is irreconcilable."

Black men had long been included in an unsegregated Navy, but no more than a token number of black soldiers had been serving in the Union army. Soon Douglass was to focus on recruitment, advocacy of equal rights for black soldiers, and protection of black prisoners of war. He was to take a special interest in a Massachusetts organization known officially as the Fifty-fourth Regiment of Massachusetts Volunteer Infantry. Too old himself to serve as a foot soldier, he would soon pass along the responsibility for fighting to his two older sons.

1 8

PATH OF GLORY

ORTY-FIVE-year-old Massachusetts governor John A. Andrew, short, rotund, and curly haired, was a man of boundless charm and energy. Like Douglass, he was motivated by a belief that untested black Americans could and would become courageous soldiers; and, like Douglass, he saw the participation of black men as part and parcel of a victory that so far had eluded Union generals.

Soon after issuance of the Emancipation Proclamation, Andrew went to Washington and obtained an order giving him permission to recruit black Massachusetts regiments. The Fifty-fourth Massachusetts was to be the first of these. Andrew was determined that its ranks be filled with young, healthy, and intelligent recruits who had led productive lives. He hoped that the Fifty-fourth's enlisted men could be supervised by at least a few black officers, but it was decided that, at least at first, the regiment would be commanded by white men.*

Andrew persuaded young and privileged Robert Gould Shaw, a Harvard dropout who as a captain had fought bravely at Antietam, to

---

*Secretary of War Edwin M. Stanton, who had authorized recruitment, promised that as black enlisted men proved themselves in combat, they would be promoted. Black men were, however, slow to be promoted and were destined to engage in a long fight for equal pay.

accept the rank of colonel and command the pioneering regiment. Andrew appointed slim and energetic businessman George L. Stearns to initiate recruiting of enlisted men. Stearns, himself a wealthy man, soon raised money to support the effort. He chose Frederick Douglass as his first paid recruiting agent. Douglass went to work without delay. His two older sons, Lewis and Frederick Jr., became his first recruits. Later, his third son, Charles, would become a recruiting agent in the South. It was no easy thing for Lewis to enlist. He was in love with Amelia Loguen and did not want to leave her.

In the bleak midwinter days of 1863, in the halls and churches of Rochester, Douglass started by

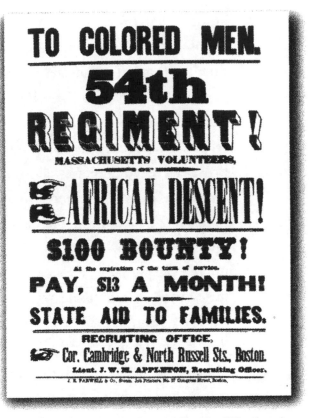

Douglass recruited black men for the Fifty-fourth Massachusetts Regiment, the first black regiment raised in the North. His eldest son served as a sergeant major of the regiment.

reminding black men that throughout recorded history they had fought for their freedoms and convictions. He invoked the names of black heroes, men like Toussaint L'Ouverture and Joseph Cinqué.* He pointed out the practical advantages of enlisting black men in the services; he

---

*On July 2, 1839, in Cuban waters, African Joseph Cinqué led a successful mutiny aboard the Spanish slave ship *Amistad*. At the end of August, the ship was discovered lying at anchor off the east end of Long Island. Cinqué and several other mutineers were taken to nearby Connecticut and in a long ensuing legal battle, were defended by a host of abolitionists. Eventually, the case was heard by the U.S. Supreme Court, where the closing arguments were delivered by John Quincy Adams. The mutineers were set free and Cinqué returned to his home in Africa.

argued that the rebel army had put slaves to work as cooks, grooms, teamsters, orderlies, and laborers. Confederate officers, thinking of the horrors that attended slave revolts, had ruled against putting firearms in the hands of black men. But it was obvious that the Confederacy had gained a conspicuous advantage from the labors of its slaves.

Still in Rochester on March 21, Douglass spoke to an audience of prospective volunteers, telling them that "when the first rebel cannon shattered the walls of [Fort] Sumter and drove away its starving garrison, I predicted that the war then and there inaugurated would not be fought out entirely by white men. . . . A war undertaken and brazenly carried on for the perpetual enslavement of colored men, calls logically and loudly for colored men to help suppress it."

He continued, "I will not argue. To do so implies hesitation and doubt, and you do not hesitate. You do not doubt. The day dawns; the morning star is bright upon the horizon! The iron gate of our prison stands half open. One gallant rush from the North will fling it wide open, while four millions of our brothers and sisters shall march out into liberty."

In recruiting for the Fifty-fourth, Douglass traveled mostly in New York State, but it soon became apparent that it would be necessary to go far afield to fill the ranks of both the Fifty-fourth and two more projected regiments. Accordingly, Douglass campaigned in the West and, eventually, in Canada. By the spring of 1863, Stearns had in hand one thousand men, some of whom were ready for combat.

Training was being carried forward at Camp Meigs, in Readville, Massachusetts—a place of open fields and lightly wooded hills, on the Boston and Providence railroad line. Shaw reported that his men showed every sign of becoming brave and loyal soldiers. Eager to present a favorable impression to what he called "the outside world," he avoided emphasizing negatives. In fact, several of his men deserted and now and then fights broke out among recruits. But Shaw never found it necessary or desirable to exert extraordinary discipline. Sometimes he confined a man to prison, but he never thought of whipping or in any way abusing anyone in his command. In fact, increasingly, his men regarded him as a just and efficient officer. They were soon to realize that he was brave as well.

Both Lewis and Charles Douglass trained at Readville, but by the time the regiment was ready, Charles was sick and couldn't go. Later, he transferred to the Fifth Massachusetts Cavalry. Lewis, clearly a strong leader, was appointed sergeant major of the Fifty-fourth.

The day before the Fifty-fourth left Readville, Frederick Douglass, Governor Andrew, and other dignitaries and family members, gathered in a trampled field that was used as a parade ground. Following preliminary speeches, Andrew gave a long address, after which he turned to Shaw and said, "I know not, Mr. Commander, when, in all human history, to any given thousand men in arms there has been committed a work at once so proud, so precious. . . ." As he handed Shaw the national and regimental flags, he made a prediction. Referring to the Stars and Stripes, he said, "Wherever its folds shall be unfurled, it will mark the path of glory."

Lewis and Charles Douglass.

On May 28, Frederick Douglass met the regiment in Boston. The men were resplendent in clean uniforms, decorated with brass buttons and belt buckles. They carried rifles fitted with brightly polished steel bayonets. Lewis Douglass led the closely ordered ranks of men who followed Shaw, who was mounted on a horse, to the top of Beacon Hill. Andrew greeted them again, this time on the steps of the State House. From there, accompanied by Gilmore's Marching Band, Shaw led his men down Beacon Street, which was flanked on one side by the lawns and trees of Boston Common and on the other by a row of redbrick houses.

This sculpture, designed and executed by Augustus Saint-Gaudens, honors Robert Gould Shaw and the men of what was known officially as the "Fifty-fourth Regiment of Massachusetts Volunteer Infantry," the first black regiment recruited in the North. Lewis Douglass served as sergeant-major in the Fifty-fourth.

The sidewalks along the route of the march were alive with enthusiastic crowds of men, women, and children waving flags, cheering their departing heroes. The Boston police were out in force, guarding against racist incidents, but though there must have been disapproving faces in the crowd, there were no unwelcome demonstrations.

Turning at the Charles Street Gate, where Frederick Douglass waited for his son to pass, the regiment marched across Boston Common and headed toward Battery Wharf, where it was to board the steamer *De Molay*, which would take them to South Carolina.

Most of the people in the crowd were white. Some, both black and white, were celebrated abolitionists. Former slave Harriet Jacobs, who had suffered grave indignities in bondage in the South, was justly proud as she watched the passage of the regiment. "How my heart swelled with the thought that my poor oppressed race were to strike a blow for Freedom!"

Frederick Douglass walked behind the regiment to Battery Wharf, where he went aboard the *De Molay,* so that he could have a few words with his son. Amid the tumult on the waterfront—the shouts of linesmen and the sounds of bells and whistles—the two men began a private conversation. Frederick Douglass stayed onboard the *De Molay* as she left the wharf. Then, before the transport left the harbor, he climbed down a rope ladder to a tug and watched the transport disappear in the haze that hung above the bay.

The regiment voyaged south to the Sea Islands, disembarking in the Port Royal region,* where it encamped on St. Helena and was given further training. On July 8, the men of the Fifty-fourth boarded the familiar *De Molay,* which took them north to the islands south of Charleston.

In the evening of July 18, 1863, Lewis Douglass followed Colonel Shaw as the Fifty-fourth attacked Fort Wagner, a giant earthwork on Morris Island, just across a narrow channel from Fort Sumter. Shaw was killed in the attack, as were many of his officers and men, before the remaining officers were compelled to call retreat.

Charlotte Forten, who knew Shaw and several of his officers and men, was doubling as a nurse in a military hospital in Port Royal. She wrote in

---

*Port Royal is an island off the coast of South Carolina. Port Royal Sound—first seen by a European in 1521—had been invaded by a fleet of federal warships in the fall of 1861, after which Union troops occupied several islands in the region and made raids on the mainland.

her diary, "To-night comes news oh, so sad, so heart sickening. It is too terrible, too terrible to write. We can only hope it may not all be true. That our noble, beautiful young Colonel is killed, and the regt. cut to pieces! . . . Thank Heaven! they fought bravely!"

After the regiment regrouped and encamped on the south end of Morris Island, Lewis Douglass wrote to Amelia Loguen, who was by then his fiancée, telling her about a preliminary fight on an island close to Morris Island and about the engagement at Fort Wagner:

Dead black soldiers at Fort Wagner. This sketch, by Frank Vizetelly, was done the morning after the July 18, 1863, attack on the earthwork.

My Dear Amelia: I have been in two fights, and am unhurt. . . . Our men fought well on both occasions. The last was desperate [. W]e charged that terrible battery on Morris Island known as Fort Wagner, and were repulsed with a loss of [many] killed and wounded. I escaped unhurt from amidst that perfect hail of shot and shell. . . . Should I fall in the next fight killed or wounded I hope to fall with my face to the foe. . . . My dear girl I hope again to see you. I must bid you farewell should I be killed. Remember if I die I die in a good cause. I wish we had a hundred thousand colored troops [so] we would put an end to this war.*

The bravery of the Fifty-fourth at Wagner, together with the heroism of both freed slaves and free black men on the lower Mississippi—at Port Hudson and Milliken's Bend—changed the attitude of white people in the north toward enlistment of black men in the Union army.

In May, following the battle at Port Hudson, a reporter for the then conservative *New York Times* wrote that "official testimony settles the question [of whether or not] the negro race can fight."

In June, Assistant Secretary of War Charles A. Dana said that "the bravery of the blacks in the Battle at Milliken's Bend completely revolutionized the sentiment of the army with regard to the employment of negro troops."

After peace had been declared, the *New York Tribune* published praise for the Fifty-fourth's accomplishment at Fort Wagner. "It is not too much to say that if this Massachusetts Fifty-fourth had faltered when its trial came, two hundred thousand colored troops for whom it was a pioneer would never have been put into the field. . . . It made Fort Wagner such a

*His wish came true. By the end of the war, two hundred thousand black men had served in the federal forces.

name to the colored race as Bunker Hill has been for ninety years to the white Yankees."

At the same time, Lincoln said that participation of black soldiers in the armies of the North tipped the balance toward a Union victory.

In July, as Lewis retreated from Fort Wagner, Lincoln and the members of his cabinet had begun to hope for victory in a war that covered a vast territory. The battle at Antietam Creek had been regarded as a turning point. Ten days before the Fifty-fourth's attack on Fort Wagner, the greatest single battle of the Civil War had been fought at Gettysburg, Pennsylvania. It had taken three full days to exhaust the combatants and the battle in that sleepy Pennsylvania town had been as indecisive as Antietam. For a second and last time it had driven General Lee away from Maryland—with devastating losses. At the same time, in the West, Union general U.S. Grant's campaign to control the Mississippi River Valley had approached completion when the Confederate garrison at Vicksburg, which had long been under siege, surrendered.

As the men of the Fifty-fourth had advanced toward Morris Island, racial violence terrorized the people of New York. The trouble had begun on March 3, when Congress had passed the Conscription Act, which stated that a man of military age, if threatened by the draft, could escape from service by providing a fit substitute or by paying the federal government a fee of three hundred dollars.

The people most affected by this law were recent immigrants—some Scandinavian and German, but most of them Irish—men much like those who had threatened and assaulted Douglass when he worked in Maryland. For more than three months after passage of the act, resentment simmered.

Anger erupted in full force on July 13, when outraged citizens broke down the doors of an armory on Second Avenue, stole firearms and ammunition, and set fire to the building. Armed, they sallied forth, rounded up several hundred followers, and, joined by countless other miscreants, began a destructive three-day riot—later known as the draft riots.

Instead of taking out their bitterness on the legislators who had passed the unjust law, the rioters directed their attacks at innocent black people, known abolitionists, antislavery journalists, and men they saw as symbols of authority. The rioters set fire to several buildings, among them the "colored orphan asylum" on Fifth Avenue between Forty-second and Forty-third Streets, the provost marshal's office on Third Avenue, and, in a burst of anti-Semitism, broke the windows in a synagogue. They torched private houses, most of them owned or occupied by black people. Policemen were murdered when they sought to tame the rioters. Federal regiments and state militias were brought into play, but were often overpowered. Innocent black men were hung from lampposts and the limbs of trees and their bodies set afire.

Douglass was in Philadelphia when the riots started. His friend Ottilie Assing was in Hoboken, and looking

The burning of the Second Avenue Armory during the draft riots in New York City in July 1863.

east across the Hudson, she could see the smoke and flames that rose above the burning buildings. As the second day of rioting began, she read about the tragedy, and reasoning that a prominent black abolitionist would have no chance of surviving the most vicious riot in the history of New York, she sent Douglass a telegram, warning him to stay away from the city.

When at last the riots ended, Assing, in her role as journalist, took a ferry to New York and walked the city's streets. She went up Fifth Avenue and stood staring at the charred and ruined orphanage. Assing's biographer tells us that some children were still living in the building and that toys were scattered on the sidewalk.

A month or so after the draft riots ended, Lewis—in camp on Port Royal—took sick. He was apparently so weakened by his illness that he couldn't faithfully perform his duties. Sick soldiers and some of the ailing teachers—people who, like Charlotte Forten, were engaged in educating former slaves—went north to recuperate. Accordingly, Lewis went to New York City, where he languished several weeks in a military hospital.

While he was recuperating, Ottilie Assing went to see him every day. When he could, Frederick Douglass visited his son, sometimes with Amelia Loguen. During this period, Assing grew fond of Lewis. She wrote that he was "an educated and pleasant young man."

Lewis soon recuperated, rejoined his regiment, and took part in subsequent engagements in the South, including the still reenacted battle of Olustee, Florida. He was mustered out of military service on May 10, 1864.

1 9

IN THE PRESENCE
OF AN HONEST MAN

EAGER AS he was to help shape public policy, Douglass often traveled to his nation's capital. The great black leader's heart may well have skipped a beat or two as his train pulled into Baltimore, where he had lived and suffered prejudice and violence. So widespread was sympathy with the Confederate cause in Baltimore that at the beginning of the war, Union troops, coming from triumphant passages through Boston and New York, had been attacked and several had been killed.*

Washington was under almost constant siege following the firing on Fort Sumter. The White House, which had the air of a rundown country mansion, was on what amounted to a swamp—a breeding ground for mosquitoes, some of which were carriers of malaria, a debilitating, often fatal, disease. Until the spring of 1862, when slavery was outlawed in the District of Columbia, slaves had been kept in pens and bought and sold in the nation's capital.

Douglass's most influential friend in Washington was Senator Charles Sumner, who had always been an unrelenting enemy of slavery.

*The march of the Sixth Massachusetts Regiment through Baltimore had brought on a full-scale riot in which four soldiers were killed and thirty-six wounded. Twelve civilians were also killed and many others wounded. This was the first official bloodshed of the war.

The White House, as it looked in Lincoln's time: circa 1860. The greenhouse was built in 1857 and was destroyed by fire ten years later.

In 1855, before Sumner was attacked by Preston Brooks, Douglass had written to him, saying, "I thank God that talents and acquirements so high as yours, are devoted to the service of my crushed and bleeding race."

In the days when the two men were often seen in each other's company, they must have presented a conspicuous contrast. Douglass was a rugged man. A crease between his nose and his forehead gave him an aggressive look. He wore his clothes as well as any man, but there was nothing of the dandy in him. Sumner, on the other hand, gave no sign of ever having labored with his hands. He wore meticulously tailored clothes and bright-colored vests, some of which were covered with embroidered flowers.

More important than their differences, most of which were superficial, was their absolute agreement on the most important issue of the day. When they talked of slavery, they never had to argue over its morality, but instead discussed their strategies for ending it. For example, in a time when it looked as if the North might lose the war, they had worked almost in tandem to persuade Great Britain not to recognize the Confederate government. By 1863, Sumner had become a friend of Lincoln and had paid frequent visits to the White House. He had sometimes mentioned Douglass to the president, who had listened patiently to the frequent criticisms leveled at him, in his paper and his speeches, by the great black abolitionist. In fact, Lincoln, never one to hold a grudge or seek revenge, was curious about the younger man.

At a time when Douglass was preoccupied with the welfare of black servicemen, he sought an interview with Lincoln so that he could talk with him about the treatment of black prisoners of war, equal opportunity for promotion of black soldiers, and equal pay. He was especially eager to make sure that if black prisoners were hanged, shot down in cold blood, or sent into slavery, the president would retaliate by ordering the execution of a rebel soldier.

Douglass was introduced to Lincoln by Senator Pomeroy of Kansas. The two men went together to the cluttered room that served as Lincoln's office. Referring to the extraordinary length of Lincoln's legs, Douglass later wrote, "When I entered he was seated in a low chair, surrounded by a multitude of books and papers, his feet and legs extended in front of his chair. On my approach he slowly drew his feet in from the different parts of the room into which they had strayed, and he began to rise, and continued to rise until he looked down upon me, and extended his hand and gave me a welcome. I began, with some hesitation, to tell him who I was and what I had been doing, but he soon stopped me, saying in a sharp, cordial voice, 'You need not tell me who you are, Mr. Douglass.'"

The two men were not of the same race, but they had much in common. Both had been curious enough in childhood to teach themselves to read and write. Both had been born with a genius for expressing complicated thoughts in simple language. True, both were creatures of their time and sometimes spoke in ways unfamiliar to us now, but both were capable of transcendent eloquence.

Lincoln invited Pomeroy and Douglass to sit down. Pomeroy was silent while Douglass started to explain the purpose of his visit. Later, he remarked, "I at once felt myself in the presence of an honest man—one whom I could love, honor, and trust without reserve or doubt."

When Douglass raised the question of retaliation for war crimes, Lincoln reminded him that two weeks earlier he had signed an order promising that in response to the killing or enslavement of black soldiers, he would order "retaliation upon the enemy's prisoners in our hands." However, paradoxically, Lincoln added that the thought of executing any man for an act committed by another man was "revolting to his feelings." The order then became an empty threat; even in the face of the wholesale slaughter of black troops following a battle at Fort Pillow, an outpost on the Mississippi River, Lincoln never could bring himself to order execution of a man who had not stood trial and been proved guilty of a crime.

Continuing his conversation with the president, Douglass asked that black soldiers be awarded equal pay and be given quick promotion when they earned it. He asked that some of them become commissioned officers. On these points, Lincoln, who was eager to avoid wholesale riots and desertions on the part of deeply prejudiced white soldiers, hesitated to commit himself. In regard to the need for black men to prove themselves worthy of promotion, he said, "Remember this, Mr. Douglass; remember that Port Hudson, Milliken's Bend, and Fort Wagner are recent events, and that these were necessary to prepare the way."

Douglass was inclined to understand Lincoln's need to compromise. "Mr. Lincoln listened with patience and silence to all I had to say. He was serious and even troubled by what I had said and by what he himself had evidently before thought upon the same points. He, by his silent listening not less than by his earnest reply to my words, impressed me with the solid gravity of his character."

It is impossible to determine how much Douglass's requests had to do with Lincoln's later actions, but it should be noted that increasingly, black soldiers were promoted and some did become commissioned officers.

As Douglass and Pomeroy rose to leave the White House, Pomeroy told Lincoln that Secretary of War Stanton had decided to make Douglass a recruiting officer under General Lorenzo Thomas,* who was enthusiastically recruiting black men in the Mississippi Valley.

Back in Rochester, Douglass was so sure that he would be granted a commission that he suspended publication of *Douglass' Monthly.* Eventually, Stanton did write to him, asking him to report to Thomas, but did not make him an officer. Douglass never blamed Lincoln for what seemed to him an insult, but it may well have been the president who denied the commission. In any case, Douglass was too proud to do the work as an ordinary citizen. He never did become an officer, though in 1865 his former colleague, Martin R. Delany, would become a major and the highest ranking black man in the Union army.

---

*Thomas raised great numbers of black soldiers, who fought bravely in the West. Many other black men would soon join in the fighting in Virginia, serving under General U. S. Grant, who had been consistently in favor of black participation in the military.

In the spring of 1864, Lincoln was nominated in a national Republican convention, held in Baltimore, to run for a second term. But several candidates were in the field, including the still popular McClellan. And considering the public's disenchantment with the progress of the war and the growing drive for peace at any price, it looked as if Lincoln might lose the election in November. In a speech later quoted many times, Lincoln made a plea for continuance of his administration, saying that he was not the greatest or the best man in America, but that the people might judge that it was best "not to swap horses while crossing the river."

Although Douglass liked and admired the president, at first he opposed his reelection on the grounds that he was slow in implementing the provisions of the Emancipation Proclamation. He was soon to change his mind.

Following his nomination, Lincoln looked back on a host of disappointments in the East—a standoff at Antietam, a failure to follow up on what had amounted to a draw at Gettysburg, and defeats at Fredericksburg and Chancellorsville. True, General Ulysses S. Grant had been responsible for successes in the West—notably the fall of Vicksburg, which had given him control of the Mississippi River. Accordingly, Lincoln had appointed him commander of all the Union armies, with headquarters in Virginia. But in July, preoccupied with capturing the Confederate capital at Richmond, Grant had left Washington largely undefended, and the capital had been menaced by Confederate soldiers who had moved northward in the Shenandoah Valley and had crossed the Potomac in the shallows northwest of the city.

On August 19, in response to an invitation from the president, Douglass went a second time to the White House. As the two met again,

Union admiral David G. Farragut was completing a victorious campaign in Mobile Bay. But at this stage, it still wasn't altogether clear that the North would win the war.

Douglass saw right away that the president was in a highly agitated state of mind. In fact, he was in an agony of indecision caused by a conflict between deeply held personal convictions and his need to compromise as to retain the loyalty of border states and the loyalty of soldiers who were serving in his armies. On closer scrutiny, Douglass realized that the president was near exhaustion. Lincoln greeted him as a friend, then lost no time in pleasantries.

Horace Greeley, using his prestige as publisher of the powerful *New York Tribune,* had taken it upon himself to suggest negotiation of a peace, asking Lincoln to arrange for a safe conduct for a team of representatives of the Confederacy, so that they could meet him at Niagara Falls, New York, and talk about an armistice.

Lincoln was willing to consider a negotiated peace, but where slavery was concerned, he was not at all prepared to

In the above cartoon, the woman, called "Mrs. North," represents public sentiment in the North when Douglass paid a second visit to the President. In mourning for the lives lost in the war, she is saying, "Mr. Lincoln, we have failed utterly in our course of action. I want peace . . . " She encourages the President to negotiate an armistice and threatens to defeat him in his bid for a second term.

compromise, so he had written what is known as his "To Whom It May Concern" letter, which had been released July 18. It said in part:

> Any proposition which embraces the restoration of peace, the integrity of the whole Union, and the abandonment of slavery . . . will be received and considered.

It was his refusal to consider any compromise involving slavery that had most infuriated Democrats and right-wing Republicans, people who had never wanted to engage in an antislavery war. Hoping to retain power long enough to finish all the work that lay ahead of him, Lincoln had composed a second letter, thinking it might put a stop to the kind of criticism generated by the letter he had written in July. Trusting and admiring Douglass as he did, he picked up a copy of the second letter and, in his penetrating tenor voice, read aloud to him.

Lincoln was a man who stood by his decisions, but in making these decisions, he was often prey to hesitation, if not excruciating doubt. In this case, abandoning the force and purpose of his "To Whom It May Concern" letter, he had written that even if he wanted to, he was incapable of waging an effective antislavery war. The people, he declared, would not support him if he did.

Douglass understood that the president needed popular support to stay in office, but was surprised by the tone of apology in the second letter. When Lincoln asked if he should release what he had read aloud, Douglass said, "Certainly not. It would be given a broader meaning than you intend to convey; it would be taken as a complete surrender of your antislavery policy, and do you serious damage."

Lincoln never sent the letter.

Douglass made allowances for his harried and exhausted president. He was pleased, perhaps even honored, that the president had sought him out and had asked him for advice on so critical a question.

Next, Lincoln gave voice to a doubt about the durability of his Emancipation Proclamation. It was, he implied, a war measure. It would lose authority once the enemy surrendered. It is not surprising, then, that Lincoln would soon after urge the passage of a Constitutional amendment that would put an end to slavery. "What he said on this day," Douglass wrote, "showed a deeper moral conviction against slavery than I have ever seen before, in anything spoken or written by him."

That day, before Douglass left the White House, Lincoln asked him to submit to him a plan to encourage more and more slaves to escape from their masters and come into Union lines. He said, "All with whom I have thus far spoken on the subject, concur in the wisdom and benevolence of the idea, and some of them think it practicable. Every slave who escapes from Rebel States is a loss to the Rebellion and a gain to the loyal cause."

Douglass lost no time in submitting such a plan, but as he was writing it, transforming military action was in progress in the South. A large portion of the nation's population—black people who had suffered all their lives what Douglass had himself endured only in his year with Covey—listened, hushed and expectant, to the rumors of a great avenging army coming south to set them free.

2 0

FREE AT LAST

TWO WEEKS after Douglass talked a second time with Lincoln, General Sherman, with one hundred thousand men, including cavalry, marched south, captured the proud city of Atlanta, and prepared to march east to the shores of the Atlantic. Sherman's campaign was unique in the annals of the Civil War. "To make war," the red-haired and fiery Sherman said, "we must and will harden our hearts. . . . Know that war, like the thunderbolt, follows its laws and turns not aside even if the beautiful, the virtuous and charitable stand in its path."

Indeed, there was something to be said for Sherman's tactics. More lives had been lost in timid operations like those of McClellan's than in sweeping operations carried out at lightning speed.

There were outstanding differences between Grant and Sherman, differences whose results would echo throughout history. Grant favored use of black men in his regiments. Sherman, who was charming and attentive in his dealings with black people, didn't want them in his army. Port Hudson, Milliken's Bend, and Fort Wagner weren't enough to make him reconsider. "With my opinion of negroes and my experience, yea, prejudice, I cannot trust them yet."

This is not to say that there were no black people following and, to some extent, taking part in Sherman's march from Atlanta to the sea, the kind of march envisioned years before by John Brown and Frederick Douglass.

Following the torching of Atlanta and the exodus of most of its white civilians, Sherman left the city smoldering and took his raggle-taggle legions toward Savannah. As Union soldiers foraged and moved on, abandoned slaves left their plantations and marched east with the soldiers who had freed them; and when the Yankee column was attacked, those among them who had stolen muskets or could borrow rifles, fired at the Confederate soldiers. Some of them helped put the torch to houses, stables, barns, and slave quarters, anything that stood along the line of march.

In Savannah, Sherman was greeted by Union soldiers who had come in from the sea two years before and had occupied Fort Pulaski. As he moved north into South Carolina, he bypassed Charleston. After setting fire to buildings in Columbia, South Carolina, he continued north again, aiming to join up with Grant.

It is fortunate that no black soldiers fought in Sherman's army as he carried out its mission. Had black soldiers been responsible for the torching and the looting of large cities in the South and the suffering of thousands of good southern citizens, their actions would have further fueled the fires of racial prejudice.

Douglass paid close attention to the presidential campaign, in which Lincoln was, by then, running against his former general George McClellan—whom he had dismissed. Douglass had had reservations about Lincoln, but Lincoln was, as Douglass put it, at least a man "of antislavery reputation." Mostly because of Sherman's victories, Lincoln won the election overwhelmingly.

This cartoon, titled "Long Abraham a Little Longer," reflects Lincoln's victory in 1864.

On March 4, 1865, a damp and windy day, Douglass, who had arrived in Washington the day before, put on his best suit and hat and walked behind Lincoln's carriage as it made its way up Pennsylvania Avenue from the White House to the Capitol. Later, he remembered, "At that time the Confederate cause was on its last legs. . . . I did not know exactly what it was, but I just felt as if [the president] might be shot."

Douglass stood by the east front of the Capitol, in a throng of onlookers, one of whom, we are told, was actor John Wilkes Booth, who was soon to gun down Lincoln. As the president appeared, the people in the crowd—women in mud-streaked dresses and men in their glistening hats and soggy suits—greeted him. "Cheer upon cheer arose, bands blatted upon the air, and flags waved all over the scene."

As Lincoln, his vice president, Andrew Johnson, and attending dignitaries stood for a moment scanning the great multitude, Lincoln spotted Douglass. "He saw me standing near by, and I could see that he was pointing me out to Andrew Johnson. Mr. Johnson, without knowing perhaps that I saw the movement, looked quite annoyed that his attention should be called in my direction. So I got a peep into his soul. As soon as he saw me looking at him, he assumed rather an amicable expression. . . . I felt that, whatever else the man might be, he was no friend to my people."

Since Johnson had delivered a long and maudlin speech inside the Capitol, the crowd outside was spared another. The president stepped forward with a printed version of his address in hand. As he prepared to speak, the clouds parted and sunlight illuminated his dark face. Then, in his penetrating voice, he delivered his short message.

Having been elected to a second term and hoping that the war was all but won, he felt free to reveal his thoughts on slavery. He said that slavery had caused the war. Then he answered all the objections to his prolonging the war in a single forceful paragraph:

> Fondly do we hope—fervently do we pray—that this mighty scourge of war may speedily pass away. Yet, if God wills that it continue, until all the wealth piled by the bond-man's two hundred and fifty years of unrequited toil shall be sunk, and until every drop of blood drawn with the lash shall be paid by another drawn with the sword, as was said three thousand years ago, so still it must be said "the judgments of the Lord, are true and righteous altogether."

Douglass wrote, "For the first time in my life, and I suppose the first time in any colored man's life, I attended the reception of President Lincoln on the evening of the inauguration." As Douglass approached the White House, carriages were pulling up to the curbstones. Men were uniformly dressed in black suits, crisp white shirts, dark cravats, and tall hats. The women's velvet and silk dresses—their skirts supported by exaggerated hoops—were in dark colors or harmonious pastel shades.

Douglass was in for a rude awakening. "As I approached the door

I was seized by two policemen and forbidden to enter. I said to them that they were mistaken entirely in what they were doing, that if Mr. Lincoln knew that I was at the door he would order my admission, and I bolted by them. On the inside, I was taken charge of by two other policemen." As these men started to eject him, Douglass called to

Detail of a painting by Peter F. Rothermel of the East Room of the White House. The artist wrote, "The scene is laid at the second inauguration." Following the threat of ejection from the mansion, Douglass made a brief appearance at the gathering; Lincoln, who had ordered his admittance, greeted him, openly and warmly, saying, "Here comes my friend Douglass." In the painting, General U.S. Grant stands behind Lincoln's shoulder, on his right. Lincoln's new Vice President, Andrew Johnson, stands on Lincoln's left.

another guest to intervene. "Just say to Mr. Lincoln that Fred Douglass is at the door."

Lincoln acted promptly; Douglass was escorted to the East Room, where the party was in progress. "A perfect sea of elegance, too, it was. The ladies were in very fine attire, and Mrs. Lincoln was standing there. I could not have been more than ten feet from him when Mr. Lincoln saw me; his countenance lighted up, and he said in a voice which was heard all around: 'Here comes my friend Douglass.'" The president asked for Douglass's opinion of his speech and Douglass said, "Mr. Lincoln, that was a sacred effort."

Later, Douglass wrote, "In all my interviews with Lincoln I was impressed with his entire freedom from popular prejudice against the colored race. He was the first great man that I talked with in the United States freely, who in no single instance reminded me of the difference between himself and myself, of the difference of color. . . . I felt as though I could go and put my hand on his shoulder."

In a postscript to his remarks on his friendship with the president, Douglass wrote that he had always heard that Mary Lincoln never quite sympathized with her husband's antislavery views, but that something she had done confirmed her loyalty. "When Mr. Lincoln died and she was leaving the White House, she selected his favorite walking cane and said, 'I know of no one that would appreciate this more than Fred Douglass.' She sent it to me at Rochester, and I have it in my house to-day, and expect to keep it there as long as I live."

On April 9, 1865, Robert E. Lee surrendered to Ulysses S. Grant at Appomattox Court House in Virginia, ending the Civil War.

2d Edition.

LEE SURRENDERS

Glory to God in the Highest:

Peace on Earth, Good will

Amongst Men.

Headline signaling the end of war.

John Wilkes Booth shot Lincoln at Ford's Theatre on the evening of April 14. The president never regained consciousness. He died at 7:22 the following morning.

Douglass was at home on April 15, when he heard the news. Mayor Daniel Moore called a meeting in Rochester's City Hall so that he and other city fathers could remark on the loss of the man who had led the people through the Civil War and, at last, freed the slaves held in bondage in America's Southland. Douglass walked alone to the center of the city and pressed through a throng of mourners to gain entrance to the hall. He sat on a bench at the back of the auditorium while several ministers eulogized the fallen president. It wasn't long before someone noticed Douglass and called out for him to speak. A friend remembered that "his name burst upon the air from every side, and filled the house."

Douglass's remarks were brief. Of Lincoln's death, he said in part, "I feel it as a personal as well as national calamity." He spoke of Lincoln's "elevation" of a people whose forebears had been captured and brought to America from Africa. Then Douglass emphasized the need for all Americans to renew and strengthen their democracy. "I feel that though Abraham Lincoln dies, the Republic lives." The distressed and grieving people in the hall cheered this optimistic affirmation of the strength of their form of government.

He continued, "Though that great and good man, one of the noblest men to trod God's earth, is struck down by the hand of the assassin, yet I know that the nation is saved and liberty established forever."

Before he finished speaking, Douglass quoted the long sentence he had so admired in Lincoln's Second Inaugural Address, the sentence signaling the president's determination to end slavery in America and fight on, if necessary, "until every drop of blood drawn with the lash shall be paid by another drawn with the sword."

Although Lincoln didn't live to see the ratification of the crucial Thirteenth Amendment to the U.S. Constitution, he had been instrumental in its passage through the Congress, instrumental in persuading the required three-quarters of the states to ratify it. The amendment was short and unequivocal:

> Section 1. Neither slavery nor involuntary servitude, except as punishment for crime whereof the party shall have been duly convicted, shall exist within the United States, or any place subject to their jurisdiction.

> Section 2. Congress shall have power to enforce this article by appropriate legislation.

The Thirteenth Amendment, ratified on December 6, 1865, spelled the end of Douglass's long crusade against the institution that might have well have crushed him in his youth.

For a while, he considered giving up speaking and writing on behalf of his beleaguered people, but he soon realized that President Andrew Johnson was incapable of following in Lincoln's footsteps, that he would obstruct black people in their quest for equal rights. In fact, under Johnson, former slaves were driven off the plots of land that the federal government had given them and, through passage of state laws that were, to say the least, devious, were rendered destitute and, in many cases, forced to go to work for former masters.

No wonder Douglass saw the need for further effort on his part. He was still in his forties and as energetic as he had been all those many years before in Nantucket. He had already given up publication of his papers, but decided to continue speaking out for his people and for what in Britain he had called "the great family of man."

EPILOGUE

ON JULY 12, 1891, Douglass was visited by a reporter for *The New York World*. Douglass had by then been living many years in a mansion on a large estate in Anacostia, an almost rural part of the District of Columbia. He was married to his second wife, Helen Pitts, a white woman.

As the reporter drove up a long and winding road to the house, he saw Douglass playing croquet with his wife and several friends. There was no mistaking Douglass, whose white hair surrounded his dark face and extended to his shoulders. He hailed the reporter, dropped his mallet, and strode energetically across his wide green lawn. The reporter remembered, "Holding out his hand to assist me from the wagon, Douglass said, 'You are welcome. I have always found the *World* truthful and uniformly just.'"

Frederick Douglass in his later years.

Before the interview began in earnest, Douglass said that he was often criticized for dissatisfaction with his lot, for feathering his already ample nest. This, his critics seemed to say, was incompatible with his campaign for the improvement of the lives of the poor black people in America, especially those in southern states.

Volunteering a response to his critics, he gestured toward his house, his garden, and a stretch of lightly wooded land and asked, "What can the world give me more than I already possess?" He continued, "I am blessed with a loving wife, who in every sense of the word is a helpmate, who enters into all my joys and sorrows. I have children whose every aim is to do me credit. I have friends loyal and true, whose great delight seems to be to gather close around me. What more can I want?"

Douglass saw no need to justify his way of life, no need to be ashamed of playing croquet, of living in luxury on an estate called Cedar Hill. In short, he believed that he had paid his dues.

Biographers have found it difficult, if not impossible, to plumb the depths of Douglass's extraordinary character. He was a generous and forgiving man. He praised the many people who had helped him live his life and do his work: those who had bought his freedom, others who had financed his crusade against slavery in America and injustice everywhere. But he spoke and wrote about his emotions only in a formal way; we can judge him only by his acts.

When he talked with the reporter from the *World,* he had less than four years left to live. He had already come to terms with death; he reckoned that the final chapter of his life had begun with the end of slavery in America, after which he had lived a "life of victory, if not complete, at least assured."

Victory for Douglass had meant not only the achievement of his public goals but the elimination of his debts and the ownership of land. His first, short memoir had been a financial triumph, but his later, longer ones had been failures, as had his newspaper ventures. Increased financial independence, and eventual prosperity, had come with an extension of his lecture tours, for which he earned substantial fees, and appointment to posts in the federal government.

Especially in his middle years and later life, Douglass was perpetually criticized for his willingness to compromise. He had been faulted for abruptly changing his interpretation of the United States Constitution. He had been severely criticized for overlooking Lincoln's failure to retaliate in kind for the killing of black prisoners of war, and for lending his support to passage of the Fifteenth Amendment to the U.S. Constitution, giving men the right to vote without regard to "race, color, or previous condition of servitude," but not mentioning a woman's right to the franchise.

In fact, as he grew older, Douglass was increasingly less idealistic, more pragmatic. But he cannot be criticized for a lack of loyalty to his children, and he deserves high praise for his capacity to forgive his masters and his former enemies.

His daughter Annie's death pained Douglass all his life. But the birth of Rosetta's daughter Annie, who resembled her namesake, must have given him great pleasure. Douglass had four children who survived their early years and eventually he had twenty grandchildren, all of whom he loved and cherished. In short, in his later years, he became the family man he had not been in his youth or middle age.

His generous, loving character was best revealed in his steadfast loyalty to his siblings, some of whom may have been no more than his half

Douglass's granddaughter Annie *(top)*, named for his youngest child who died when she was ten years old, and her mother Rosetta Douglass Sprague *(bottom)*.

brothers and half sisters. In 1867, he returned to Maryland and was reunited with Eliza, one of his two older sisters.* Eliza, married to a man named Peter Mitchell, had nine children.

In 1867, a letter came to Douglass in Rochester from his brother, Perry Downs, who had spent fifty years in slavery and had been brutally assaulted at Holme Hill Farm by the cruel and drunken Andrew Anthony. Perry's wife, Maria, and his children had been "sold south," while he had remained enslaved in Maryland. Following his emancipation, he went south to find his family; having discovered them, in Brazos County, Texas, he was working as a field hand and was being "treated pretty well," but was eager to come north.

Douglass wrote to Perry, and after a delay of several months, Perry wrote again, this time from New Orleans. Douglass arranged for passage for his brother and his family to Rochester. Douglass wrote, "The meeting of my brother after nearly forty years of separation is an event alto-

* Douglass was the fourth child in a family of seven. His brother, Perry Downs, was the first. His oldest sister, Sarah, was "sold south" in 1832. Following emancipation, Frederick heard from Sarah, but they never saw each other in their later years. Eliza was his other older sister. Frederick's younger sister Kitty later moved to Washington. There is no record of the lives and deaths of Frederick's other younger sister, Arianna, or of Harriet, whom he had seen at Holme Hill Farm in 1826 and believed might be another of his mother's children.

gether too affecting for words to describe." He added, "How utterly accursed is slavery, and how unspeakably joyful are the results of its overthrow!"

Douglass was widely praised for his generosity toward his brother. He built Perry and his family a small house on his land in Rochester and helped him learn the skills that he would need to lead an independent life.

The Douglass children didn't share their father's love for the Downs family. Raised in association with white people and with members of the black elite, they were horrified by the appearance of these relatives. Remarking on reports from Rochester, Douglass's second son, Charles, who was working at the Freedmen's Bureau in Washington, D.C., wrote to his father, "I don't understand in what way those people you have at home are related to you. Is it that Mr. Downs is your half brother? For what I have heard of their conduct I should be afraid even to have them in the same neighborhood."

This was certainly a most constricted view of a man who was probably his father's brother; and, because the Freedmen's Bureau was created to assist and educate people much like Perry and the members of his family, it is all the more remarkable that Charles so lacked an understanding of his father's wish to nurture them.

In any case, the Downs family couldn't stand Rochester winters. They moved back to the Eastern Shore, where they lived until their children went their separate ways, after which they moved to Washington.

Douglass was no less faithful to his friends and colleagues. Having celebrated a reunion with Amanda Auld and established a friendship with her husband, he went often to their house in Philadelphia. He maintained a close friendship with Charles Sumner and reestablished his friendship with William Lloyd Garrison.

• • •

At the end of 1870, when Douglass moved to Washington, leaving his wife, Anna; his oldest child, Rosetta; Rosetta's husband, Nathan Sprague; and their four children in Rochester, he began the final chapter of his life, the one commented on by the *New York World* reporter.

He was in Washington on the night of June 2, 1872, when his Rochester house caught fire. Everyone was asleep when the fire began to spread. Rosetta was "awakened by the odor of smoke and a bright light in the room." She roused Nathan, who ran through the corridors alerting Anna and the children. Rosetta took her baby in her arms and went outside while Nathan guided others down the stairway. Outside, after seeing that all the members of the family were safe, Nathan noticed that the barn was burning. He rescued their cart horse but was forced to leave the cow to perish.

Anna, Rosetta, and the children watched as Nathan and the members of a fire brigade brought out some furniture and a piano from the gathering inferno. The heat was so intense that everyone fell back a hundred yards or more and stood by as the house collapsed.

Rosetta sent a telegram to Douglass, telling him that everyone had been rescued. Following an agonizing railroad journey to Rochester, Douglass met the members of his family, who were staying with neighbors, then surveyed the blackened ruin of his house. Most of the furniture, every steel engraving, and every photograph had been destroyed. Letters, notes, and financial records lay in ashes, as did a complete file of *The North Star* and the other Douglass newspapers published in Rochester.

Douglass, believing that the fire had been set by racists, in what he called the "spirit of the Ku Klux Klan," moved his family to Washington, where, for three years or so, he continued publication of another paper—this one called *The New National Era,* in which he had bought an interest.

There were many times when Douglass might have returned to the Eastern Shore, but something always held him back. At last, on June 17, 1877, he returned to St. Michaels. After he had talked with some of his Bailey cousins, he walked to a redbrick house on Cherry Street, where he called on Thomas Auld, the master who had sent him back to the cruel Edward Covey. Auld was lying in his bed, too sick to rise. Then eighty-two, he knew that his time was short. Perhaps because he knew that death was imminent, Auld wept openly. Douglass was too moved to speak. Later, Douglass wrote that he could see that Auld was ready to "depart in peace."

Washington, D.C., as it was in 1868.

Having heard about his visit to St. Michaels, Ottilie Assing wrote to Douglass. Still very much in love with him, as she would be to the end, she began regretfully, "If only for once I could see the Eastern Shore in your company!" Then she criticized his behavior. She wrote that his forgiveness of his former master weakened his position as a spokesman for his people. Assing's criticism was an indication that their relationship was cooling, not because she loved him less but because he was growing tired of her.

On a chilly January day in 1878, Douglass took a train from Washington to Philadelphia, where he visited Amanda Sears for the last time. Amanda knew that she was dying and had asked to see him so that he could talk with her again about her mother, who had played so pivotal a role in his escape from slavery. Following a short visit, Douglass left. A week later, he received a note from Sears, telling him that Amanda had died peacefully. Sears added, "God bless you for your kindness to her." It was in the fall of that same year that the Douglass family moved from central Washington to Cedar Hill, in Anacostia.

In 1881, Douglass visited the Lloyd plantation and was taken through the grounds by Edward Lloyd V's great-grandson. Seeing that Aaron Anthony's substantial house behind Wye House looked much as he remembered it, he walked into its large kitchen, and, standing still for a moment, paid his respects to the place where he had last seen his mother, where she had defended him from the cruel Aunt Katy and had presented him with a heart-shaped ginger cake.

Anna Douglass, who had long been ailing, had a stroke in 1882 that left her partially paralyzed. On August 4, she died at Cedar Hill and was buried in Mt. Hope Cemetery in Rochester. Thereafter Douglass suffered from acute depression. He felt as if he had killed the woman who had borne his children and had done so much for him in his youth and middle years. A year later, still depressed, he spent a summer with good friends in Maine, then returned to Washington, where he reestablished a friendship with Helen Pitts, who lived with her uncle in a house on land adjoining

Cedar Hill and had worked for Douglass when he was recorder of deeds for the District of Columbia.

Less than two years after Anna's death, Douglass married Pitts, who was twenty years his junior. Pitts had qualities in common with both Julia Griffiths and Ottilie Assing. All three were attractive. All were white, and all were intelligent. Pitts was strong enough and proud enough to brush aside the storm of criticism generated by a mixed marriage in a time of deep prejudice against black Americans. She had also brushed aside the German woman who eight years or more before had begun to lose her hold on Douglass.

Douglass and Pitts were married by Francis Grimké in Washington's Fifteenth Street Presbyterian Church. Grimké's wife, Charlotte Forten, who had kept so beautiful a diary of her months as a teacher of freed children in South Carolina, stood by the loving couple.

At Cedar Hill, following the ceremony, the four Douglass children greeted their new stepmother. They had loved their mother and had grown fond of Assing, so were troubled by their father's second marriage.

Further awkwardness awaited Douglass when he and his wife visited her family in Honeoye Falls, New York, not far from Rochester. Pitts's father, Gideon, had been an abolitionist. He had met Douglass several times years before and had admired him, but because he had known both Julia Griffiths and Ottilie Assing, he thought Douglass something of a rake and refused to let him in.

Douglass had been criticized for visiting and forgiving Thomas Auld. Now he was roundly criticized for marrying a white woman. Some friends refused to speak to him. Others found fault with him openly for putting love ahead of his career. In an editorial, the black *Pittsburgh Weekly News*

Ida B. Wells as she was when Douglass knew her. She was a fine and loyal friend.

declared, "We have no further use for him. His picture hangs in our parlor; we will hang it in the stables."

The beautiful and articulate Ida B. Wells, who was leading a campaign for federal action against lynchings in the South, came to Douglass's defense. She wrote that, like most of her colleagues, she "would have preferred that Mr. Douglass had chosen one of the beautiful, charming colored women of [her] race for his second wife." But, Wells said, "He loves Helen Pitts and it is outrageous that they should be crucified by both black and white people."

Douglass expressed his appreciation to Wells, telling her that she and Charlotte Forten were the only women of their race who had given him support.

While he was on his honeymoon in Canada and New England, Douglass learned that Ottilie Assing had committed suicide. He must have been sickened by the news. It was not as if he and Assing had engaged in a short and secret dalliance. He had loved her through two turbulent and critical decades. They had walked together arm in arm in the streets of some of the great cities of America. She had expressed affection for his children and been tolerated by his wife. He knew that years before their relationship had cooled she had made a will that favored him—giving him semiannual income from a small trust fund and leaving him some of her most treasured books and her gold pens. In her will she had written that her testament was made "in recognition of his noble labors in the antislavery cause." He later learned that she had kept the will intact.

After hearing of the suicide, Douglass must have thought back to their meeting in Rochester, to their nights together in Hoboken, one of which had prompted her to remark in a letter to her sister, "We had the most exquisite time together and made plans for the summer."

Douglass knew that she had loved him, knew that until his second marriage, she had hoped that he would marry her. How did he cope with what must have been an avalanche of guilt?

He was aware that suicide was celebrated in German folklore, literature, and song. He knew that years before he had met her, Assing had attempted suicide, stabbing herself several times in the chest. He didn't know, but chose to believe that she had been suffering from cancer. He wrote to a friend of his, "She . . . always maintained her right in case of being afflicted with an incurable disease to save herself the pain of a lingering death and her friends the trouble of caring for her."

After he returned to Cedar Hill, Douglass learned details of Assing's death: In the weeks before she died, she had been living in the Hotel d'Espagne, in Paris. On the afternoon of August 21, 1884, she walked to the Bois de Boulogne—a vast public park east of the Seine—and sat down on a bench in a wooded area. There, within the sound if not the sight of bridle paths and crisply dressed pedestrians, she swallowed a small dose of potassium cyanide and died almost instantly.

• • •

In the fall of 1886, Douglass and his wife sailed to England, where they visited the many people who had given their support to him in his early years. One of these was Julia Griffiths, who had written to him, wishing them a happy life.

From England, they went on to Paris, where they spent two months before they made extensive tours of France, Italy, Greece, and Egypt. After they returned to England, Helen sailed from Liverpool to New York, while Douglass stayed on to revisit Ireland and Scotland. His taste for almost frantic travel might be judged as an escape from meditation on a life that had begun to wear a little thin.

Tired as he may have been, Douglass's later lectures were much more than frosting on a cake. As late as 1888, he spoke forcefully on behalf of black people in the South—people who were suffering untold hardship following the breakdown of Reconstruction—a program begun by Lincoln to restore the southern states to "their proper practical relation to the Union" and, at the same time, protect the interests of freed slaves.

On April 16 of that year, Douglass gave a speech called "In Law Free, in Fact a Slave," a bitter statement of a truth that in the century to follow would become a cry of outrage on the lips Martin Luther King Jr.

Douglass talked about the relation "between the colored people and the old master class of the South." Almost a quarter of a century after the emancipation of the slaves, he saw a continued effort by "the old master class" to reestablish a caste system, and he judged the effort a success.

The freed people were paid no more than a pittance and were therefore often forced to steal the food they needed for themselves and their children. "I admit," Douglass said, "that the negro, and especially the plantation negro, the tiller of the soil, has made little progress from bar-

barism to civilization, and that he . . . is worse off, in many respects, than when he was a slave. . . . But I contend that the fault is not his. . . . He is the victim of a cunningly devised swindle, one which paralyzes his energies, suppresses his ambition, and blasts all his hopes; and though he is nominally free he is actually a slave. I here and now denounce his so-called emancipation as a stupendous fraud—a fraud upon him, a fraud upon the world. It was not so meant by Abraham Lincoln."

He went on to explain the nature of the swindle. "Free" men and women not only were not paid a living wage but were paid in handwritten "scrip"—receipts to be redeemed only in a general store, often owned by their employers. Some storekeepers charged outrageous prices for the goods they sold to their black customers. In any case, the system left field hands destitute, unable to afford to leave their neighborhoods, much less travel to a city in the North. "A blind man," Douglass said, "can see that the laborer is by this arrangement bound hand and foot."

In 1889, Douglass, by then widely thought of as an elder statesman, was appointed minister resident and consul general to the Republic of Haiti, which shares the island of Hispaniola with the Dominican Republic. Having toured the Dominican Republic in 1871, Douglass knew Hispaniola well* and knew something of its history, especially that involving the great Haitian leader Toussaint L'Ouverture.

Haiti's capital, Port-au-Prince, overlooks the Golfe de la Gonâve, a vast natural harbor that in the eighteenth century had sheltered ships whose holds were filled with slaves brought in chains from Africa. Haiti was and would remain a hotbed of racial and political unrest. Large and

---

*Douglass had gone to Hispaniola in 1871 as a member of a commission sent by then president Ulysses S. Grant to investigate the possibility of annexation of the Dominican Republic.

powerful European nations had fought over it and two racial groups—blacks and mixed races—were in constant competition there.

In July, when Douglass and his wife arrived in Port-au-Prince, President General Florvil Hyppolite was in control. Hyppolite wore white suits and blue-tinted glasses. He was an educated person, a member of the black elite, but was soon to be revealed as a cold and ruthless man.

Douglass was expected to persuade Hyppolite to allow the U.S. Navy to construct a coaling and refitting station in a Haitian seaport. Hyppolite spoke no English. Douglass spoke no French, but through an interpreter, he managed to establish cordial personal relations with the Haitian ruler.

In spring and summer, Haiti suffers vicious winds, sudden and torrential rains, and unbearable humidity. The heat is often merciless. Although Douglass and his wife lived in a villa overlooking carefully tended gardens and lush vegetation, Port-au-Prince soon became a hell on earth for both of them. His wife was weakened by the climate and in July of 1890, Douglass took a leave of absence so that they could go back home to Cedar Hill.

While President Benjamin Harrison argued with his advisers over policy and over Douglass's effectiveness, Douglass and his wife remained in Washington, not returning to Port-au-Prince until the end of 1890.

In May of 1891, Douglass witnessed an uprising during which Hyppolite rode a horse through the streets and ordered the wholesale slaughter of his enemies. As he led his soldiers in suppressing the insurgents, his hat fell off. This was taken by his superstitious people as a sign that evil lay in store for him. In fact, five years later, he fell off his horse as he was suffering a fatal heart attack.

Douglass failed in his mission to acquire a naval base in Haiti. Clumsy and aggressive moves by the U.S. Navy had antagonized the Haitians, and Hyppolite feared the presence of a foreign government.

Despite the failure of his mission, Douglass chose to believe that his appointment to a diplomatic post had brought honor to his race. But because he was opposed to the use of military force in expanding U.S. power, he was called unpatriotic. When he was attacked by racists—people who implied that he had failed because black people were inferior to whites—he replied evenly, "This color argument is not new. It besieged the White House before I was appointed." Amid a barrage of criticism, he and his wife again returned to Washington, where Douglass formally resigned his post.

Less than a year before he died, Douglass went back to his birthplace. His grandmother's cabin was no longer standing. When a reporter asked him why he had returned, he said, "I came to drink water from the old-fashioned well that I drank from many years ago, to see the few old friends that are left of the many I once had, to stand on the old soil once more before I am called away by the great Master, and to thank Him for His many blessings to me during my checkered life."

At noon on February 20, 1895, Douglass went to a meeting of the National Council of Women, held in Washington. At the end of the proceeding, he was escorted to the platform by his friend and colleague Susan B. Anthony. There he made a few remarks and was given an ovation. It was growing dark when he returned to Cedar Hill.

At supper, he talked with his wife about the meeting. He had always been a skillful mimic and had often parroted the speeches of his friends. As he began to imitate a suffragette, he stopped, clutched at his chest, collapsed, and died.

The most celebrated black man of his century, Douglass was eulogized in Washington's A.M.E. Zion Church, where a friend sang a verse appropriate to the occasion:

Lay him low, lay him low
Under the clover or under the snow;
How we loved him none can know;
Lay him low.

He was buried next to his first wife Anna and his younger daughter, Annie, in Rochester's Mount Hope Cemetery. There are monuments to him in Rochester and in Washington, D.C., but there are none of any consequence on the Eastern Shore of Maryland. Wye House and its gardens and dependencies, where Douglass spent several agonizing years in his childhood, are much admired, as are many other unintentional monuments to slavery.

BIBLIOGRAPHICAL
ESSAY

AS I BEGAN work on this book, I knew something of the places and the period in which Frederick Douglass lived his life. I had sailed the waters of the Chesapeake and explored the creeks and estuaries of the Eastern Shore of Maryland. I knew Boston and the Massachusetts seacoast and had sailed several times from the mainland to Nantucket, where my narrative begins. I had crossed the North Atlantic many times on merchant ships. I knew the British Isles less well than Douglass did, but I was at home in London. To me, Rochester was a far and foreign city, but I was welcomed warmly there. I had lived in New York City and had read its history. I was born in Washington, D.C., and knew the city well. I had visited Hispaniola.

In this essay and the notes that follow it, I refer my readers to the names of authors and editors listed in my bibliography. I include first names when I have listed two or more authors with the same last name. Otherwise, I use last names only. References to the "biographies" point the way to the authors of the best biographies of Douglass: Philip S. Foner, Huggins, McFeely, Preston, Quarles, and Washington. References to the "autobiographies" point to Douglass's memoirs, all of which are now available in a single volume, edited and with an introduction by Henry Louis Gates Jr. See Douglass.

As I worked on this book, I made constant use of general histories and black histories of the nineteenth century, especially books about the Civil War. For general histories, see Catton, Churchill, Commager, Franklin, and McPherson, all of whom are listed in my bibliography. For black histories, see Aptheker, Bennett, Brown, DuBois, Foner, Livermore, McPherson, Quarles, and Ripley.

Dickson Preston, who died in 1985, wrote about my subject's childhood and his youth and, in preparing to do so, dug deeply into long-neglected archives in Maryland: in Oxford, St. Michaels, Annapolis, and Baltimore. It was Preston who established, beyond a shadow of a doubt, the month and year of Douglass's birth and unearthed and verified many details that relate to Douglass's forbears. The only detailed sources on his early life are Douglass's memoirs. Gates has said that these contain exaggerations and internal contradictions, but lacking any further source, I have made extensive use of my subject's published memoirs and his papers.

The most important woman in Douglass's life was his first wife, Anna. Because Anna was illiterate, she left no record of her own. Douglass's daughter, Rosetta, wrote, "It is difficult to say anything of mother without the mention of father, her life was so enveloped in his."*

While Anna was alive, the second most important woman in Douglass's life was German journalist Ottilie Assing. In his memoirs, Douglass mentions Assing only in a formal way. I learned most of what I wrote about

---

*Rosetta added, "Few of their earlier friends in the North really knew and appreciated the full value of the woman who presided over the Douglass home for forty-four years." She went on to say something far less complimentary. "The reserve in which she held herself made whatever she might attempt of a jocose nature somewhat acrid."

Assing from a thorough and reliable biography of Assing, published in 1999. See Diedrich.

Throughout the writing of this book, I made wide use of guidebooks published by the Writer's Project of the Works Progress Administration—which was established in 1935. These guidebooks contain delightful histories.

In most cases, I relied on other scholars for quotations from newspapers and periodicals. For papers published on the Eastern Shore of Maryland, see Preston. I did make use of microfilm editions of *The Liberator* and *The New York Times,* found at the Williams College Sawyer Library, and a file of *Harper's Weekly* at the Sawyer. For the *Baltimore American,* the *Baltimore Sun,* the Boston *Chronotype,* and the *National Anti-Slavery Standard,* I referred to Eric Foner, Philip S. Foner, McFeely, and Preston. In interpreting Anna Douglass's enigmatic character, I leaned heavily on Rosetta Douglass Sprague's "Anna Murray-Douglass—My Mother as I Recall Her." This essay appears in *The Journal of Negro History,* Vol. 8, Issue 1 (January 1923), pages 93–101. Also useful was a collection of privately printed letters to Douglass from his children. See Cooper.

NOTES ON SOURCES

CHAPTER 1: NANTUCKET

Douglass's first memoir, *Narrative of the Life of Frederick Douglass,* contains a preface by William Lloyd Garrison, in which Garrison describes Douglass's Nantucket speech. For the history of Nantucket, see Stevens and Lancaster.

CHAPTER 2: THOSE SONGS STILL FOLLOW ME

It must be said at the outset that without the work of Dickson Preston, who lived on the Eastern Shore of Maryland and doggedly investigated Douglass clues and documents, it would have been almost impossible to reconstruct Douglass's childhood and youth. See Preston. For Maryland histories, see Browne and Brugger.

CHAPTER 3: OH, HAVE MERCY!

This chapter, including as it does the brutal whipping of a woman slave, is based on the autobiographies. Gates has, in effect, suggested that Douglass's memoirs are partly fictional. Among the memoirs, there are certainly exaggerations and internal contradictions, but in writing what was clearly antislavery propaganda, Douglass did not exaggerate agonies of the kind endured by many slaves throughout the South. Other slaves have documented the conditions under which they lived and toiled, as have white antislavery southerners. See Browne, Brugger, Katz, Kemble, Preston, and Yentsch.

CHAPTER 4: LOOK UP, CHILD

Annapolis was the first city Douglass saw and Baltimore the first metropolis. In 1826, Baltimore was a flourishing seaport and shipbuilding city. Many books document the city's growth. See Hall, Owens, and Ridgely.

CHAPTER 5: TALL OAKS FROM LITTLE ACORNS GROW

In this chapter, I took the liberty of supplying a verse from the Book of Job, found in the King James Version of the Holy Bible. The verse I chose may or may not have been the one read aloud by Sophia Auld. I have used several of the many editions of *Uncle Tom's Cabin,* but have used only the first edition of *The Columbian Orator.* See Bingham. For biographies of the brave and colorful Daniel O'Connell, see Macintyre and Moley. For Nat Turner, see Oates. For John Quincy Adams, see Nagel.

CHAPTER 6: THE DARK NIGHT OF SLAVERY

We have only Douglass's accounts of his stay in St. Michaels. However, I am familiar with the town and the surrounding countryside and waterways.

CHAPTER 7: TAKE HOLD OF HIM!

I found Douglass's account of his fight with Edward Covey almost incredible. No doubt Frederick fought with Covey, but it was unlikely that the fight lasted two nights and three days, so I took the liberty of calling it "long and bitter combat." Incidentally, Preston doubts that Thomas Auld was as cruel as Frederick says he was.

CHAPTER 8: WE ARE BETRAYED

As in other early chapters, I relied on the autobiographies, on Preston's work, my memory of the Eastern Shore, and narratives of slavery as practiced there and in other places on or near the Chesapeake. See Browne, Brugger, Douglass, and Yentsch.

CHAPTER 9: ANNA

In describing Anna's character, I found it necessary to do some guesswork based on her generous actions and the writings of Rosetta Douglass Sprague. Also see Cooper. I have found only one photograph of Anna, taken when she was much older and probably much heavier than she was when Douglass married her. In his autobiographies, which together fill at least one thousand printed pages, he mentions Anna only twice, both times as "my intended wife." The second time, he adds that they "were married by Rev. James W. C. Pennington."

CHAPTER 10: ALL ABOARD!

In writing my account of Douglass's escape from Baltimore, I used the autobiographies. Through study of maps, and railroad and steamboat posters of the period, I was able to reconstruct his journey to New York. As I described his arrival in New York, I was in familiar territory. Here I used my memory and histories and guidebooks of New York.

CHAPTER 11: BECAUSE YOU ARE BLACK

For Garrison, see Mayer, Merrill, and Nye. For Forten, see Remond, Whittier, and Burchard. For Douglass's travels and his efforts to desegregate New England railroad cars, see the autobiographies. For Phillis Wheatley, see Wheatley.

CHAPTER 12: THE GREAT FAMILY OF MAN

For information on Douglass's first passage on the *Cambria,* see Hyde and Babcock. For Dublin, see Chart and Pritchett. For Manchester, see Messenger. For O'Connell, see Macintyre and Moley.

CHAPTER 13: WHAT HAVE WE TO DO WITH SLAVERY?

For Douglass's battle with the Free Church of Scotland, see Douglass, especially *Liberating Sojourn.* I scanned countless books on London and read some of them. Especially useful were guidebooks of the period, found in the Williams College Sawyer Library. Also, see Fox. For articles of and amendments to the U.S. Constitution, including the Bill of Rights, see James MacGregor Burns, et al. For the speeches in Finsbury Chapel and the London Tavern, see Douglass, edited by Blassingame; and Douglass, edited by Philip Foner. Charles Dickens's life and works are readily available, as are the speeches of Martin Luther King Jr.

CHAPTER 14: *THE NORTH STAR*

For New York State, and Rochester in particular, see guidebooks and histories of the period, especially those relating to the Hudson River, the Genesee River, and the Erie Canal. For details of Rochester history, I used maps and steel engravings of the city. For particulars about Garrison, see Mayer, Merrill, and Nye. As mentioned earlier, a set of microfilm editions of *The Liberator* is on file at the Williams College Sawyer Library. For *The North Star* and Douglass's other newspapers, see Douglass, edited by Blassingame. Serious scholars will benefit from a visit to Rochester libraries, especially the collections at the University of Rochester and the Rochester Historical Society. For Gerrit Smith, see Harlow and Renehan. For the New York City underworld in the eighteenth century, and information about ward boss Isaiah Rynders, see Asbury.

CHAPTER 15: LET WOMAN TAKE HER RIGHTS!

In describing Worcester, Massachusetts, I relied on several visits to the city. Also, I referred to local histories. For Lucretia Mott, Abby K. Foster, and Lucy Stone, see Harper and Douglass: *Frederick Douglass on Women's Rights*. For Sojourner Truth, see Gilbert. For the Gorsuch incident, see Douglass, edited by Blassingame. For *Uncle Tom's Cabin*, see Stowe. There are dozens of editions of Stowe's novel published in several languages. My quotations from the book were taken from the first 1852 edition. For Douglass's speech about the Fourth of July—delivered on July 5—see Douglass, edited by Blassingame. For the controversy over Julia Griffiths, see *The Liberator* and Douglass, edited by Blassingame. Information about "Border Ruffians," the sack of Lawrence, Kansas, and John Brown's activities came from Boyer, DuBois, Renehan, and Scott. For the Assing and Douglass affair, see Diedrich. For Toussaint, see general works and Rodman.

CHAPTER 16: A STEEL TRAP

For information on John Brown and accounts of his raid on Harpers Ferry, see the general histories mentioned in my bibliographical essays. Again, see Brown's biographers mentioned in my notes on Chapter 15. See Douglass's own accounts of his relationship with Brown. For the Secret Six, see Renehan. For Douglass's many visits to Hoboken, New Jersey, see Diedrich. For notes on Virginia's governor Henry A. Wise, see Boyer, DuBois, McFeeley, and Renehan. For Douglass's first visit to Amanda Sears, see the autobiographies. For notes on Virginia's governor Alexander H. Wise, see Boyer, DuBois, Philip Foner McFeely, and Renehan. For Isaac and Amy Post, see the autobiographies; Douglass, edited by Blassingame; and Harper. For Douglass's daughter Annie's sickness and her death, see the records of the Mt. Hope Cemetery, in Rochester.

CHAPTER 17: GOD BE PRAISED!

For Rosetta's comments on her sister's death, see Cooper. For "The Battle Hymn of the Republic," see Boatner. For Douglass's changing views on Lincoln, see Douglass, edited by Blassingame. For Lincoln's First Inaugural Address, see Lincoln and Burchard, *Lincoln and Slavery*. For Douglass's view of the address, see the autobiographies. For the firing on Fort Sumter, see general histories of the Civil War by Catton, Commager, McPherson, and others. For Senator Charles Sumner, see the autobiographies and Donald, Mayer, Merrill, and Nye. For Lincoln's Emancipation Proclamation, see Burchard, *Lincoln and Slavery;* Douglass, *The Frederick Douglass Papers;* and Franklin. For reaction of black people to the Proclamation see Forten and McPherson. for the text of the Proclamation, see Burchard, *Lincoln and Slavery*. For Douglass's recruitment of black soldiers, see the autobiographies and Blight; Brown; Burchard, *One Gallant Rush;* McPherson; and Shaw.

CHAPTER 18: PATH OF GLORY

For the activities of the Fifty-fourth Massachusetts Regiment, see the autobiographies; Burchard, *One Gallant Rush;* Forten; McPherson; Quarles; and Shaw. For Lewis Douglass's letter to his wife, Amelia, see McPherson, *The Negro's Civil War*. For the battle at Port Hudson, see Brown and the *New York Times*. For comments on the importance of the performance of the Fifty-fourth at Fort Wagner, see the *New York Tribune*. For Joseph Cinqué, see Jones. For Charlotte Forten's touching comment on the aftermath of the attack, see Forten. For the Draft Riots in New York, see Asbury, Cook, Gilje, and Werstein.

CHAPTER 19: IN THE PRESENCE OF AN HONEST MAN

For the Douglass-Sumner friendship, see Donald and Douglass, edited by Blassingame. For the first Douglass-Lincoln meeting, see the autobiographies.

For Lorenzo Thomas, see McPherson and Quarles. For an overview of Lincoln's military disappointments, see Catton, Churchill, and McPherson. For the second Lincoln-Douglass visit, see the autobiographies. For the portion of the draft of the letter Lincoln wrote to Greeley, see Douglass, edited by Blassingame. As noted in my text, the letter was not sent to Greeley, and its text is not on record.

CHAPTER 20: FREE AT LAST

For Sherman's march, see Cary, Catton, Churchill, Commager, and McPherson. For Lincoln's Second Inaugural Address, see Lincoln and the autobiographies. For Douglass's encounter with the White House police and his reaction to Lincoln's death, see the autobiographies and Douglass, edited by Blassingame. For the text of the Thirteenth Amendment to the U.S. Constitution, see James MacGregor Burns et al.

EPILOGUE

For Douglass's July 12, 1891, remarks to a reporter for the *New York World*, see Douglass, edited by Blassingame. For the Fifteenth Amendment to the U.S. Constitution, see James MacGregor Burns et al. For Douglass's reunions with his siblings, see Preston. For accounts of Douglass's relationship with his brother, Perry, see the autobiographies. For Charles Douglass's reaction to his father's nurturing of Perry and his family, see Cooper. See also the autobiographies and biographies. For the burning of the Douglass house in Rochester and the reunion with Douglass's former master, see the autobiographies, and the biographies. For Assing's letter about the reunion, see Diedrich. For Douglass's final visit to Amanda Sears and Amanda's death, see Douglass, edited by Blassingame. For Anacostia, see Hutchinson. For Douglass's visit to the Lloyd plantation, see the autobiographies and Preston. For Anna's death and Douglass's reaction to it, see Douglass, edited by Blassingame, McMurry, and Preston. For Helen Pitts, see the autobiographies and Diedrich. For Ida B. Wells' support of Douglass at the time of his marriage to Pitts, see Wells and McMurry. For details of Assing's death, her will, and Douglass's reaction to the tragedy, see Diedrich. For Douglass's later European travels, see the biographies and autobiographies. For his April 18, 1886, speech "In Law Free, in Fact a Slave," see Douglass, edited by Blassingame. For Douglass's sojourn in Haiti, see the biographies. For Haitian history, see Léger and Rodman. For Douglass's poignant visit to his birthplace, see the autobiographies.

BIBLIOGRAPHY

Aptheker, Herbert, ed. *A Documentary History of the Negro People in the United States,* 7 vols. New York: Citadel Press, 1969.

Asbury, Herbert. *The Gangs of New York.* New York: Alfred A. Knopf, 1927.

Babcock, F. Lawrence. *Spanning the Atlantic.* New York: Alfred A. Knopf, 1931.

Bennett, Lerone Jr. *Before the Mayflower: A History of the Negro in America 1619–1964.* Chicago: Johnson Publishing, 1964.

Bingham, Caleb. *The Columbian Orator.* Boston: Manning & Loring, 1797.

Blight, David W. *Frederick Douglass' Civil War.* Baton Rouge: Louisiana State University Press, 1989.

Boatner, Mark Mayo III. *The Civil War Dictionary.* New York: David McKay, 1959.

Boston City Council. *A Memorial of Frederick Douglass.* Boston: Printed by order of City Council, 1896.

Boyer, Richard O. *The Legend of John Brown: A Biography and a History.* New York: Alfred A. Knopf, 1973.

Brown, William Wells. *The Negro in the American Rebellion.* New York: Citadel Press, 1971.

Browne, William Hand. *Maryland: The History of a Palatinate.* Boston: Houghton, Mifflin, 1884.

Brugger, Robert J. *Maryland: A Middle Temperament: 1634–1980.* Baltimore: Johns Hopkins University Press, 1988.

Burchard, Peter. *Charlotte Forten: A Black Teacher in the Civil War.* New York: Crown Publishers, 1995.

———. *Lincoln and Slavery.* New York: Atheneum, 1999.

———. *One Gallant Rush: Robert Gould Shaw and His Brave Black Regiment.* New York: St. Martin's Press, 1965.

———. *"We'll Stand by the Union": Robert Gould Shaw and the Black 54th Massachusetts Regiment.* New York: Facts on File, 1993.

Burns, James MacGregor, and Stewart Burns. *A People's Charter: The Pursuit of Rights in America.* New York: Vintage Books, 1993.

Burns, James MacGregor, et al. *Government by the People.* Upper Saddle River, NJ: Prentice Hall, 2000.

Carey, John, ed. *The Faber Book of Reportage.* London: Faber and Faber, 1987.

Catton, Bruce. *The Centennial History of the Civil War,* 3 vols. Garden City: Doubleday, 1961–1965.

Chart, D. A. *The Story of Dublin.* London: J. M. Dent, 1907.

Churchill, Winston S. *The American Civil War.* New York: Fairfax Press, 1985.

Commager, Henry Steele, ed. *The Blue and the Gray: The Story of the Civil War as Told by Participants.* Indianapolis: Bobbs-Merrill, 1950.

Cook, Adrian. *The Armies of the Streets: The New York City Draft Riots of 1863.* Lexington: University of Kentucky Press, 1974.

Cooper, Mark Anthony Sr., ed. *Dear Father: A Collection of Letters to Frederick Douglass from His Children 1859–1894.* Philadelphia: Fulmore Press, 1990.

Diedrich, Maria. *Love Across Color Lines: Ottilie Assing and Frederick Douglass.* New York: Hill and Wang, 1999.

Donald, David Herbert. *Charles Sumner and the Rights of Man.* New York: Alfred A. Knopf, 1970.

_____. *Lincoln.* New York: Simon & Schuster, 1995.

Douglass, Frederick. *Autobiographies: Narrative of the Life of Frederick Douglass,* first published in 1845; *My Bondage and My Freedom,* first published in 1855; *The Life and Times of Frederick Douglass,* first published in 1892. These three works are now available in one volume. New York: Library of America, 1994.

_____. *Liberating Sojourn: Frederick Douglass & Transatlantic Reform,* edited by Alan J. Rice and Martin Crawford. Athens: University of Georgia Press, 1999.

_____. *The Life and Writings of Frederick Douglass,* 4 vols., edited by Philip S. Foner. New York: International Publishers, 1950–1955.

_____. *Frederick Douglass on Women's Rights,* edited by Philip S. Foner. Westport, CT: Greenwood Press, 1976.

_____. *The Frederick Douglass Papers,* 5 vols., edited by John W. Blassingame and John R. McKivigan. New Haven: Yale University Press, 1979–1992.

DuBois, W. E. B. *Black Reconstruction.* New York: Harcourt, Brace, 1935.

_____. *John Brown.* New York: International Publishers, 1968.

Foner, Eric. *Reconstruction: America's Unfinished Revolution, 1863–1877.* New York: Harper & Row, 1988.

Foner, Philip S. *Frederick Douglass, a Biography.* New York: Citadel Press, 1964.

Forten, Charlotte L. *The Journals of Charlotte Forten Grimké,* edited by Brenda Stevenson. New York: Oxford University Press, 1988.

Fox, Celina, ed. *London—World City, 1800–1840.* New Haven: Yale University Press, 1992.

Franklin, John Hope. *The Emancipation Proclamation.* Garden City: Doubleday, 1963.

_____. *Reconstruction: After the Civil War.* Chicago: University of Chicago Press, 1961.

Gilbert, Olive. *Narrative of Sojourner Truth, a Bondwoman of Olden Time.* New York: Oxford University Press, 1991.

Gilje, Paul A. *The Road to Mobocracy: Popular Disorder in New York City, 1763–1834.* Chapel Hill: University of North Carolina Press, 1987.

Hall, Clayton Colman, ed. *Narratives of Early Maryland, 1633-1684.* New York: Charles Scribner's Sons, 1910.

Hopkins, Eric. *Birmingham: The First Manufacturing Town in the World, 1760–1840.* London: Weidenfeld & Nicolson, 1989.

Harlow, Ralph Volney. *Gerrit Smith: Philanthropist and Reformer.* New York: Henry Holt, 1939.

Harper, Judith E. *Susan B. Anthony: A Biographical Companion.* Santa Barbara: ABC-CLIO, 1998.

Huggins, Nathan Irvin. *Slave and Citizen: The Life of Frederick Douglass.* Boston: Little, Brown, 1980.

Hutchinson, Louise Daniel. *The Anacostia Story, 1608–1930.* Washington: Smithsonian Institution Press, 1977.

Hyde, Francis E. *Cunard and the North Atlantic, 1840–1973.* Atlantic Highlands, NJ: Humanities Press, 1975.

Jones, Howard. *Mutiny on the Amistad: The Saga of a Slave Revolt and Its Impact on American Abolition, Law, and Diplomacy.* New York: Oxford University Press, 1986.

Katz, William Loren, ed. *Five Slave Narratives: A Compendium.* New York: Arno Press, 1968.

Kemble, Frances Anne. *Journal of a Residence on a Georgian Plantation in 1838–1839,* edited and with an introduction by John Anthony Scott. New York: Alfred A. Knopf, 1961.

Kunhardt, Philip B. Jr., Philip B. Kunhardt III, and Peter W. Kunhardt. *Lincoln, an Illustrated Biography.* New York: Alfred A. Knopf, 1992.

Lancaster, Clay. *The Architecture of Historic Nantucket.* New York: McGraw-Hill, 1972.

Léger, J. N. *Haiti: Her History and Her Detractors.* New York: Neale Publishing Co., 1907.

Lincoln, Abraham. *Abraham Lincoln: Complete Works; Comprising His Speeches, Letters, State Papers, and Miscellaneous Writings,* edited by John G. Nicolay and John Hay. New York: Century, 1894.

Livermore, George. *An Historical Research Respecting the Opinions of the Founders of the Republic, on Negroes and Slaves, as Citizens, and as Soldiers.* New York: Arno Press, 1969.

Macintyre, Angus. *The Liberator: Daniel O'Connell and the Irish Party, 1830–1847.* London: Hamish Hamilton, 1965.

Mayer, Henry. *All on Fire: William Lloyd Garrison and the Abolition of Slavery.* New York: St. Martin's Press, 1998.

McDaniel, George W. *Hearth and Home: Preserving a People's Culture.* Philadelphia: Temple University Press, 1982.

McFeely, William S. *Frederick Douglass.* New York: W. W. Norton, 1991.

McMurry, Linda O. *To Keep the Waters Troubled: The Life of Ida B. Wells.* New York: Oxford University Press, 1998.

McPherson, James M. *Battle Cry of Freedom: The Civil War Era.* New York: Oxford University Press, 1988.

———. *The Negro's Civil War: How American Negroes Felt and Acted During the War for the Union.* New York: Pantheon Books, 1965.

Merrill, Walter M. *Against Wind and Tide: A Biography of William Lloyd Garrison.* Cambridge: Harvard University Press, 1963.

Messinger, Gary S. *Manchester in the Victorian Age.* Manchester, UK: Manchester University Press, 1985.

Moley, Raymond. *Daniel O'Connell: Nationalism Without Violence.* New York: Fordham University Press, 1974.

Nagel, Paul C. *John Quincy Adams: A Public Life, a Private Life.* New York: Alfred A. Knopf, 1997.

Nye, Russel Blaine. *William Lloyd Garrison and the Humanitarian Reformers.* Boston: Little, Brown, 1955.

Oates, Stephen B. *The Fires of Jubilee: Nat Turner's Fierce Rebellion.* New York: Harper & Row, 1975.

——. *To Purge This Land with Blood: A Biography of John Brown.* Amherst: University of Massachusetts Press, 1984.

Owens, Hamilton. *Baltimore on the Chesapeake.* Garden City: Doubleday, Doran, 1941.

Preston, Dickson J. *Young Frederick Douglass: The Maryland Years.* Baltimore: Johns Hopkins University Press, 1980.

Pritchett, V. S. *Dublin: A Portrait.* New York: Harper & Row, 1967.

Quarles, Benjamin. *Frederick Douglass.* Washington, D.C.: Associated Publishers, 1948.

——. *Lincoln and the Negro.* New York: Oxford University Press, 1962.

——. *The Negro in the Civil War.* Boston: Little, Brown, 1953.

Renehan, Edward J. *The Secret Six: The True Tale of the Men Who Conspired with John Brown.* New York: Crown Publishers, 1995.

Ridgely, David. *Annals of Annapolis.* Baltimore: Cushing and Brother, 1841.

Ripley, C. Peter, et al., eds. *The Black Abolitionist Papers,* 5 vols. Chapel Hill: University of North Carolina Press, 1985-1992.

Rodman, Selden. *Haiti: The Black Republic.* Old Greenwich, CT: Devin-Adair, 1973.

Rose, Willie Lee Nichols. *Rehearsal for Reconstruction: The Port Royal Experiment.* Indianapolis: Bobbs-Merrill, 1964.

Scott, John Anthony, and Robert Alan Scott. *John Brown of Harpers Ferry.* New York: Facts on File, 1988.

Shaw, Robert Gould. *Blue-Eyed Child of Fortune: The Civil War Letters of Colonel Robert Gould Shaw, edited and with an introduction by Russell Duncan.* Athens: University of Georgia Press, 1992.

Stevens, William Oliver. *Old Nantucket, the Faraway Island.* New York: Dodd, Mead, 1936.

Stowe, Harriet Beecher. *Uncle Tom's Cabin: or, Life Among the Lowly.* Boston: John P. Jewett, 1852.

Sundquist, Eric J., ed. *Frederick Douglass: New Literary and Historical Essays.* Cambridge: Cambridge University Press, 1990.

Washington, Booker T. *Frederick Douglass.* Philadelphia: G. W. Jacobs, 1907.

Wells, Ida B. *Crusade for Justice: The Autobiography of Ida B. Wells, edited by Alfreda M. Duster.* Chicago: University of Chicago Press, 1970.

Werstein, Irving. *July, 1863.* New York: Julian Messner, 1957.

Wheatley, Phillis. *The Poems of Phillis Wheatley, edited and with an introduction by Julian D. Mason Jr.* Chapel Hill: University of North Carolina Press, 1966.

Yentsch, Anne Elizabeth. *A Chesapeake Family and Their Slaves.* Cambridge: Cambridge University Press, 1904.

PHOTOGRAPH CREDITS & PERMISSIONS

INDEX